THE MAN WHO
WASN'T THERE
Ethan Coen & Joel Coen

faber and faber

First published in 2001
by Faber and Faber Limited
3 Queen Square London WCIN 3AU
Published in the United States by Faber and Faber Inc.
an affiliate of Farrar, Straus and Giroux LLC, New York

Photoset by Faber and Faber Ltd
Printed in England by Mackays of Chatham plc, Chatham, Kent

Ethan Coen & Joel Coen are hereby identified as authors of this work in accordance with Section 77 of the Copyright, Designs and Patents Act 1988

A CIP record for this book
is available from the British Library
ISBN 0-571-21250-6

CONTENTS

CAST AND CREW

MAIN CAST

ED CRANE	Billy Bob Thornton
DORIS CRANE	Frances McDormand
BIG DAVE BREWSTER	James Gandolfini
FRANK RAFFO	Michael Badalucco
CREIGHTON TOLIVER	Jon Polito
FREDDIE RIEDENSCHNEIDER	Tony Shalhoub
BIRDY ABUNDAS	Scarlett Johansson
WALTER ABUNDAS	Richard Jenkins
ANNE NIRDLINGER	Katherine Borowitz
JACQUES CARCANOGUES	Adam Alexi-Malle

MAIN CREW

Directed by	Joel Coen
Written by	Joel Coen
	Ethan Coen
Produced by	Ethan Coen
Executive Producers	Tim Bevan
	Eric Fellner
Co-Producer	John Cameron
Cinematography by	Roger Deakins
Film Editing by	Roderick Jaynes
	Tricia Cooke
Music	Carter Burwell
Production Design by	Dennis Gassner
Costume Design by	Mary Zophres

INTRODUCTION

One of the hallmarks of old age is the gradual realization that one is no longer conversant with, or even much aware of, the surrounding culture. Living in Hayward's Heath these past thirty years, largely retired from the movie business, I must confess that until recently I hadn't heard of – let alone seen – *Pearl Harbor*, *The Klumps* (sp.?), *Vertical Limit*, or *Lara Croft, Tomb Raider*. Well, Pearl Harbor I'd heard of, of course, in its geographic and historical sense, but the motion picture was not on my radar, so to speak. Someone told me that its star was Ben Affleck, which I asked them to repeat a number of times in the belief that they were trying to expel phlegm. Other sources confirm that such is in fact the name of a contemporary cinema star. Live and learn.

I mention this to explain my puzzlement at many of the candidates for the title of the movie whose script these remarks introduce, candidates bandied back and forth by the filmmakers as I tried to concentrate on the picture's montage. I am something in the nature of a film editor emeritus, and brothers Joel and Ethan Coen are self-styled cinéastes who had begun shooting this, their latest movie, with little concern as to what it might be called. *Pansies Don't Float* was an early working title that, thank goodness, they were prevailed upon to discard. They had likewise been coaxed away from more opaque titles aiming to peg the movie generically as a *noir*: *I, the Barber*; *The Man Who Smoked Too Much*; and *The Nirdlinger Doings*. The Coens entertained (or entertained themselves with) *Missing, Presumed Ed* and *Mr. Mum* – both references to the alienated and close-mouthed central character Ed Crane, played by William Thornton. They rejected as 'too Sixties' the one candidate of theirs that I found not uninteresting, *I Love You, Birdie Abundas!*

At first I kept my head down as they argued, struggling to make simple match cuts in footage shot by people patently ignorant of the simplest mechanics of scene construction. The chore was familiar to me, this being my seventh picture with these filmmakers, and prompted me to wonder whether a deft and resourceful film editor mightn't sometimes be less the director's friend than his enabler, licensing the sloppiness and ineptitude of he who might otherwise reform. This is a theme upon which, sadly, I could at this point write a book. Friends at Faber & Faber, take note.

As I mentioned before, I am retired. I now unsheath my scissors, as it were, only to work for *les frères* Coen. They pay well, no doubt of necessity, since their footage, or their persons, frighten away those editors not in their golden years who would be more willing to trade some salary for a feature film on the old c.v. In the case of this film, they promised to sweeten the pot with a paid holiday weekend in Blackpool if I should come up with a title they would end up using. I was happy enough to give it some thought.

Titles, I believe, should be straightforwardly descriptive. Gimmicks, whimsy, and effortful grandeur are simply not on. Accordingly, my suggestion was the direct and unfussy *Edward Crane*. Imagine my surprise when the filmmakers called as I was stuffing seaside togs into my valise, to say that they felt 'we' still hadn't 'nailed it.' I offered what I thought was a sensible amplification: *The Barber, Crane*. When this too was rejected I began to question my own decision to engage with cretins. All the more when they explained that they were looking for something poetic, like *The Other Side of Fate*, which they both found appealing but were disinclined to use because of their uncertainty as to whether Fate had more than the one side. *None Know My Name* was another of their favorites, rejected only because of its superabundance of m's and n's. They had solicited my advice, they now told me, because they thought that, being British, I might know some 'Shakespearean stuff' that 'might work.' They propounded the theory that a good title intrigues, is suggestive, allusive, and makes one want to know more. I was going to suggest *The Man with the Gas Hearth* but, mindful that they also wanted a savor of pulpy confession, proposed *My Hearth Is Gas*. This prompted a few minutes' thought from Ethan, at the end of which he asked, 'Is that from the sonnets?'

Perhaps one should not draw back the veil from the creative process. Here are two men respected in the arts about whom it is possibly not necessary to know that they are in fact clods. But on the other hand this knowledge might be tonic to a general public imbued with perhaps too much awe for creative personages. At any rate, my musings on their personal vacuity bore me to what I thought was not a bad title for their film: *The Man Who Wasn't There.*

And indeed, the brothers received it with enthusiasm. But the next day a crestfallen Ethan told me that the title had already been used: it was the name of a Steve Guttenberg comedy of the 1980s. When I asked the obvious question, to wit, 'Who is Steve Guttenberg?' Joel giggled, and Ethan stared. 'Duh,' he said. '*Police Academy*?'

Well, I will take their word that there is such a person who starred in such a movie; as I confessed at the beginning of this introduction, I am hardly an authority. At any rate, Joel proposed that, to avoid infringement, my title be amended to *The Man Who Wasn't All There.* When I pointed out that the added word, though short, significantly altered the title's meaning, Ethan bellowed that I was a 'pedant.' (Both men tend to become tart when challenged.) They came up with two other choices that I found obscure: *I Will Cut Hair No More Forever,* and the puzzlingly verbless *Ed Crane, You So Crazy!* There matters rested, in uneasy contemplation of unsatisfactory alternatives, until the two decided to 'call Steve' and ask for permission to use my clearly superior nomination.

It was a no doubt bemused Mr Guttenberg who received an incoherent phone call (I heard the one side) that began with the brothers simultaneously, fulsomely, and at length setting out how much they 'dug' his work, and ended with them asking if it would be all right if they used *The Man Who Wasn't There* as the title for a movie about a barber who really wants to be a dry cleaner and therefore many people meet violent death. Once he'd sorted out what they were after, Mr Guttenberg informed the brothers that he himself was not the proprietor of the title in question, and advised them to ring up his movie's producer, Universal Pictures.

Intimidated by the mention of Universal Pictures, they handed the matter over to the phalanx of lawyers whose full-time job it is to protect the two brothers from themselves. Securing rights in the title was achieved in one short and businesslike phone call. I had my holiday; you hold the book.

Roderick Jaynes
Hayward's Heath
June 2001

Black.

ED (V.O.)
Yeah, I worked in a barbershop. But I never considered
myself a barber . . .

We track back from a barber's pole.

. . . I stumbled into it – well, married into it more precisely . . .

*We track back from a shopkeeper's bell triggered by an opening door.
The pull back and tilt down show the top of the head of a customer
entering in slow motion.*

. . . It wasn't my establishment. Like the fella says, I only
work here . . .

*We track along a shelf backed by a mirror and holding pomade, after-
shave, hair tonic, a whisk brush.*

. . . The dump was 200 feet square, with five chairs, or sta-
tions as we call 'em, even though there were only two of us
working . . .

*We track in on a big man in a barber's smock scissoring across a lock of
hair that he pulls taut between two fingers of one hand. In slow motion,
he laughs and chats.*

. . . Frank Raffo, my brother-in-law, was the principal barber.
And man, could he talk . . . CU on mouth

*Another man in a barber's smock is running electric clippers across a
child's head. A cigarette plumes between his lips.*

. . . Now maybe if you're eleven or twelve years old, Frank's
got an interesting point of view, but sometimes it got on my
nerves. Not that I'd complain, mind you. Like I said, he was
the principal barber. Frank's father August – they called him
Guzzi – had worked the heads up in Santa Rosa for thirty-

five years until his ticker stopped in the middle of a Junior
Flat Top. He left the shop to Frankie free and clear. And that
seemed to satisfy all of Frank's ambitions: cutting the hair
and chewing the fat. Me, I don't talk much . . . *Slow motion*

He plucks the cigarette from his mouth and taps its ash into a tray.

. . . I just cut the hair . . .

LATE IN THE DAY *venetian blinds - light cast over shop*

*The barbershop is empty of customers. Late sun slants in through the
front window. The two barbers – the narrator and his brother-in-law –
sit in two of the barber chairs, idly reading magazines.*

> FRANK
> Says here that the Russians exploded an A-bomb and there's
> not a damn thing we can do about it.

> ED
> Uh-huh.

> FRANK
> How d'ya like them apples?

Beat.

> . . . Ed?

> ED
> Huh?

> FRANK
> Russians exploded an A-bomb.

> ED
> Yeah.

> FRANK
> (*shaking his head*)
> Jesus . . .

> ED (V.O.)
> Now, being a barber is a lot like being a barman or a soda-
> jerk; there's not much to it once you've learned the basic

moves. For the kids there's the Butch, or the Heinie . . .

We cut to examples of the haircuts as they are ticked off:

. . . the Flat Top, the Ivy, the Crew, the Vanguard, the Junior
Contour and, occasionally, the Executive Contour. Adults
get variations on the same, along with the Duck Butt, the
Timberline . . .

Ed trims the fringe around a balding head.

. . . and something we call the Alpine Rope Toss.

*He snips one long lonely strand of hair and carefully drapes it across a
bald pate.*

Suburban.

. . . I lived in a little bungalow on Napa Street. The place was
OK, I guess; it had an electric ice box, gas hearth, and a
garbage grinder built into the sink. You might say I had it
made.

*We float slowly toward a white bungalow on a quiet street as a black
coupe pulls into the driveway.*

. . . Oh yeah. There was one other thing . . .

frames woman

*We track in through a bedroom door to discover a woman putting on a
girdle.* looks like fatale

. . . Doris kept the books at Nirdlinger's, a small department
store on Main Street. Unlike me, Doris liked the work,
accounting; she liked knowing where everything stood. And
she got a ten per cent employee discount on whatever she
wanted – nylon stockings . . .

Close on her legs as she rolls up a stocking and clips it to the garter.

. . . make-up, and perfume . . .

*Close on an atomiser misting her bosom with Jungle Gardenia by
Tuvaché.*

. . . She wore a lot of perfume.

Doris in a flouncy dress is setting coasters on a coffee table.

. . . Doris's boss, Big Dave Brewster, was married to Ann

Nirdlinger, the department store heiress. Tonight they were coming over for dinner – as Doris said, we were 'entertaining' . . .

Ed sits on the living-room davenport in an uncomfortable suit, smoking.

. . . Me, I don't like entertaining.

[handwritten: Sits alone – isolated –]

The doorbell rings.

THE DOOR

Ed opens it to reveal a large man in a suit and his demure, bird-like wife.

> DAVE
> How ya doin', Ed?

> ED
> OK. Take your coat, Ann?

DINNER TABLE

The two couples are in the middle of the meal.

> DAVE
> Japs had us pinned down in Buna for something like six weeks. Well, I gotta tell ya, I thought *we* had it tough, but, Jesus, we had supply. *They* were eating grubs, nuts, thistles. When we finally up and bust off the beach we found Arnie Bragg, kid missing on recon; the Japs had *eaten* the sonofabitch, if you'll pardon the, uh . . . And this was a scrawny, pimply kid too, nothin' to write home about. I mean, I never would've, ya know, so what do I say, honey? When I don't like dinner, what do I say?

Ann smiles wanly.

. . . I say, Jesus, honey, Arnie Bragg – *again*?!

He roars with laughter.

Ed gives an acknowledging smile.

4

... Arnie Bragg – *again*?!   *Ed doesn't laugh*
                                sits stoney
He dries his eyes with the corner of a napkin.   *faced*

... Were you in the service, Ed?

ED

No, Dave, I wasn't.

DORIS

Ed was 4F on account of his fallen arches.

DAVE

Mm, that's tough.

FRONT PORCH

*Ed is standing alone on the porch, watching the sun go down. Crickets
chirp. From inside the house we hear laughter and clattering dishes.*
                                                          outside alone
                                                          smoking
ED (V.O.)
... Yeah ... I guess Doris liked all that he-man stuff. Sometimes I had the feeling that she and Big Dave were a lot
closer than they let on ...

He turns and looks through the screen door into the house.
                                                       framed

5

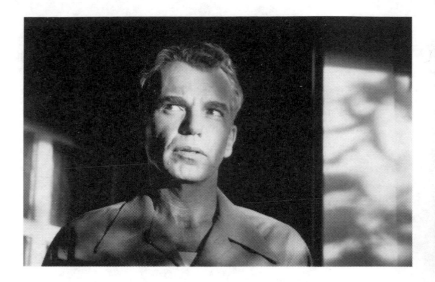

Across the dim living room we can see a sliver of the brightly lit kitchen. Big Dave, wearing a frilly apron, stands at the counter drying dishes. His broad back heaves with laughter while Doris, just hidden by the wall, chats away, handing dishes across.

. . . The signs were all there plain enough – not that I was gonna prance about it, mind you. It's a free country.

Footsteps approach the front porch.

With the squeak of the screen door, Big Dave emerges.

DAVE
Holding down the porch area?

Ed gives a half-grin of wry acknowledgment. Big Dave relaxes, fore-arms against the porch railing, gazing out at the front lawn.

. . . That's quite a wife you got there.

ED
Mm.

DAVE
She's a rare one.

                              ED

How's business, Dave?

                             DAVE

Couldn't be better. These're boom times in retailing. We're
opening another store, Big Dave's Annex, there on Garson.
This is strictly haberdashery – casual wear, pyjamas, ladies'
foundations and undergarments. Matter of fact, I'm thinking
of making Doris the comptroller. How're things at the, uh,
the barbershop?

                              ED

All right, I guess.

                             DAVE

. . . Fine. Fine. Well, you might want to drop by the Annex
when we open, update your suit – 'course, you're in the
smock all day.

He chuckles.

          . . . Say, where do you get those things anyway?

                              ED

Specialty store down in Sacramento.

                             DAVE

Uh-huh.

*There is a silence. At length, gazing out at the lawn, Big Dave clears
his throat.*

CHURCH

                           ED (V.O.)
Doris and I went to church once a week . . .

*We are tilting down a long stained-glass window depicting the resurrec-
tion of Christ.*

          . . . Usually Tuesday night . . .

Faintly, we hear an amplified voice:

                               7

I . . . seven . . .

Ed sits at a long table, staring at the window, a lit cigarette in his mouth.

. . . Bee . . . four . . .

ED (V.O.)
Doris wasn't big on divine worship . . .

Doris is concentrating on the six cards spread in front of her.

. . . and I doubt if she believed in life everlasting; she'd most likely tell you that our reward is on this earth and bingo is probably the extent of it . . .

Still focused on her cards, Doris mutters to Ed:

DORIS
Watch your card, honey.

CALLER
I . . . sixteen . . .

Ed continues to gaze off at the window, smoke pluming from his cigarette.

ED (V.O.)
I wasn't crazy about the game, but, I don't know, it made her happy, and I found the setting peaceful.

CALLER
Gee . . . nine . . .

Doris sucks in her breath.

DORIS
Jesus, bingo – BINGO!

BARBERSHOP

Sun slants in through the big window at the end of the day. Ed sweeps hair trimmings, looking intently down at the floor, a cigarette dangling from his lip. Frank sits on one of the vinyl waiting chairs, talking at Ed's back.

FRANK

. . . so you tie your own flies, Ed. I mean, if you're really seri-
ous. You tie your own flies, you do a – I know it's matickless,
I know, people say, hey, you can buy flies at the store – but
you can buy your *fish* at the store, Ed, you see what I'm saying?

ED

Uh-huh.

FRANK

The point is there's a certain art to the process. The point is
not merely to provide, and let me point out, these fish are
not as dumb as you might think.

ED

Uh-huh.

FRANK

Sportsmanship! That's my point. June fly, Ed? Mosquito?
Which of these? Well, what fish do you seek?

ED

Yeah.

FRANK

Sure, go to the store. Go there, describe to the man where
you will be fishing, and for what, and the weather conditions,
sun, no sun, whatnot, and so forth, and then you might as
well have the man go ahead and sell you the goddamn FISH,
Ed . . .

*We see a black-suited figure approaching through the windows at the
far end of the shop. He is almost blown out by the late-day sunlight hit-
ting the window.*

. . . My point is, this is a man who knows nothing no matter
how much you tell him, so sell him the goddamn FISH, Ed.

*The bell over the front door tinkles, and the swarthy middle-aged man
walks in. He is well dressed – perhaps a little too snazzily for this small
town – and has a sporty pencil mustache.*

MAN

OK, boys, which of you gets the privilege?

FRANK

We're just closing, friend.

MAN

Oh, happy days! I wish I was doing well enough to turn away business! More power to ya, brother! The public be damned!

FRANK

Hey, what's your problem, friend? This is a business establishment with posted hours –

Ed cuts in with a jerk of the head.

ED

I'll take care of him, go ahead, Frank. Have a seat, mister.

Frank looks sourly at the stranger.

FRANK

. . . You sure, Eddie?

ED

Yeah, yeah – go home.

As Frank leaves:

FRANK

In your ear, mister.

The stranger chuckles.

STRANGER

Oh, those fiery Mediterraneans. Say! Not so fast there, brother –

Ed has switched on the clippers, but the stranger waves him back; he lifts off a toupee.

. . . Pretty good, huh? Fools even the experts. 100 per cent human hair, handcrafted by Jacques of San Francisco, and I'd hate to have to tell you what I paid for it.

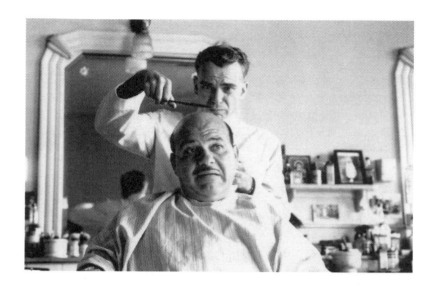

ED

Uh-huh.

STRANGER

Yes, it's a nice rug. I'm paying it down on the installment plan . . .

Ed starts to trim the stranger's fringe.

. . . A lot of folks live with the pate exposed. They say the dames think it's sexy. But for my money it's just not good grooming – and grooming, my friend, is probably the most important thing in business – after personality, of course . . .

He twists around to offer his hand.

. . . Creighton Tolliver, pleased to know ya.

ED

Ed Crane. What brings you to Santa Rosa?

CREIGHTON

A goose, friend. I was chasing a wild goose. Ed, have you ever heard of venture capital?

ED

Uh –

                    CREIGHTON

Well, it's the wildest goose there is. Risk money. Very specula-
tive. Except, Ed, in certain situations, it's not, see? I thought
I had a prospect here. Well, I make the haul up and this lousy
so-and-so tells me his situation has changed – all his capital's
gonna be tied up in expansion plans of his own. Thank you,
mother! Pop goes another bubble! It's only the biggest business opportunity since Henry Ford and I can't seem to interest a soul!

                    ED

That right.

                    CREIGHTON

It's called dry cleaning. You heard me right, brother, '*dry
cleaning*' – wash without water, no suds, no tumble, no stress
on the clothes. It's all done with chemicals, friend, and your
garments end up crisp and fresh. And here's the capper: no
shrinkage.

                    ED

Huh.

                    CREIGHTON

That's right! Dry cleaning – remember the name. It's going to
revolutionize the laundry industry, and those that get in early
are gonna bear the fruit away. All I need is $10,000 to open
my first store, then I use its cash flow to finance another, and
so on – leap-frog, bootstrap myself a whole chain. Well, me
and a partner. Cleanliness, friend. There's money in it.
There's a future. There's room to grow . . . Say, that's looking
pretty good. Let's see it with the hairpiece on . . .

BATHROOM DOORWAY

*It is evening. Ed leans against the bathroom doorjamb gazing contem-
platively off, hands thrust into his pockets, a cigarette between his lips
pluming smoke.*

ED (V.O.)

Dry cleaning . . .

The reverse shows Doris soaking in the tub, reading a magazine.

. . . Was I crazy to be thinking about it? Was he a huckster, or opportunity, the real McCoy?

in complete shadow

Ed takes the cigarette from his mouth, exhales.

. . . My first instinct was, no, no, the whole idea was nuts. But maybe that was the instinct that kept me locked up in the barbershop, nose against the exit, afraid to try turning the knob. What if I could get the money?

DORIS

Honey?

ED

Mm.

She lifts one leg and rests the heel on the rim of the tub.

DORIS

Shave my legs, will ya?

Ed saunters over, perches on the tub and puts the cigarette back in his mouth to free his hands. He picks up a bar of soap and starts soaping the leg.

He sets down the soap and picks up a safety razor.

The razor takes long slow strokes along the lather, dark bits of hair flecking the white foam.

ED (V.O.)

. . . It was clean. No water. Chemicals.

He shakes the razor in the tub. Shavings float away across the soap-slicked water.

DORIS
(*absently, as she reads*)

Gimme a drag.

Ed pulls the cigarette from his mouth between two fingers, uses the two fingers to flip it over, and holds it for Doris as she sucks.

He brings the cigarette, now marked with lipstick, back to his own mouth. She murmurs:

. . . Love ya, honey.

A DOOR

We hear a voice, muffled through the door, breaking into laughter.

A hand enters to knock.

> VOICE

Yeah, come in.

The door swings open to show Creighton in his shirtsleeves sitting on the bed, talking on the phone. A tray of room-service dishes sits near him.

He is bald; his hairpiece sits on the pillow next to him.

> CREIGHTON
> (*into the phone*)

OK . . . yeah. I'll see you tomorrow.

He hangs up, looks quizzically at Ed.

. . . Oh, I thought you were the porter . . . Can I help you?

Ed stands awkwardly by the door.

> ED

. . . I'm, uh, Ed.

The stranger's look does not show recognition.

. . . Ed Crane. Remember? Today?

> CREIGHTON

Sorry, friend, I, uh, you got me at a disadvantage.

> ED

I'm, uh, I'm – the barber.

CREIGHTON

Jesus! The barber! I'll be a sonofagun. Why didn't you say so? 'Course – the barber.

Ed nods, his smile faint and forced.

... I didn't recognize you without the smock. Did I – damn – did I leave something at the shop?

ED

No. I might be interested in that, uh, business proposition –

Creighton, surprised, quickly picks up his hairpiece and arranges it on his head.

CREIGHTON

You got the dough?!

ED

I can get it, yeah.

CREIGHTON

Come in, come in, siddown over there. Coffee?

ED

No. I – tell me –

15

CREIGHTON

Sure.

ED

What's involved, aside from putting up the money? What're you looking for the partner to do?

CREIGHTON

Do? Hell, nothing. Well, you'll want to keep tabs on your investment, of course, but I'm looking for a silent partner. I've done the research, I've contacted the vendors, the deal is set. I'm just looking for venture capital, friend. Disappear if you want, check in whenever you like – I want the dough; I don't take attendance.

ED

And how do we share –

CREIGHTON

Fifty–fifty, straight down the line. You and me. Finance and expertise. So – you've got the dough then, do ya?

ED

I'll have it in a week.

CREIGHTON

Well, I'll be damned. The barber! And I thought this trip was a bust. Well . . .

He reaches for a bottle of bonded whiskey on the night stand and hands Ed a glass.

. . . it just goes to show, when one door slams shut, another one opens. Here's to ya, uh . . .

ED

Ed.

They both knock back the whiskey. Creighton leans back and gives Ed a heavy-lidded stare, a faint smile on his lips, his hairpiece slightly askew.

Ed stares back.

After a beat, without taking his eyes off Ed, Creighton reaches up and loosens his tie. An almost imperceptible wink.

Ed stares.

. . . Was that a pass?

CREIGHTON
(*hoarsely*)

Maybe.

ED

You're out of line, mister.

Creighton throws up his hands apologetically.

CREIGHTON

No problem!

ED

Way out of line.

CREIGHTON

Right! Strictly business.

ED

Yeah.

CLOSE ON TYPEWRITTEN NOTE

It says:

I KNOW ABOUT YOU AND DORIS CRANE.
COOPERATE OR ED CRANE WILL KNOW.
YOUR WIFE WILL KNOW. EVERYONE WILL
KNOW. GATHER $10,000 AND AWAIT
INSTRUCTIONS.

A hand pulls the note out of a typewriter carriage.

ED (V.O.)

I sent it to Dave the next morning. And I waited.

BARBERSHOP

We are looking down at the top of an eight-year-old's crew cut as clippers buzz its perimeter.

...ds a magazine. The youngster reads a comic as Ed works his head.

                              ED
Frank.

                              FRANK
Huh?

                              ED
This hair.

                              FRANK
Yeah.

                              ED
. . . You ever wonder about it?

                              FRANK
Whuddya mean?

                              ED
I don't know . . . How it keeps on coming. It just keeps grow-ing.

                              FRANK
Yeah – lucky for us, huh, pal?

                              ED
No, I mean it's growing, it's part of us. And we cut it off. And throw it away.

                              FRANK
Come on, Eddie, you're gonna scare the kid.

Ed shuts off the clippers and gives the apron a flap.

                              ED
OK, bud, you're through.

The kid hops down, still reading his comic, and ambles out the door. Ed gives Frank a considering stare.

          . . . I'm gonna take his hair and throw it out in the dirt.

FRANK

What the –

ED

I'm gonna mingle it with common house dirt.

FRANK

What the hell are you talking about?

Ed turns back to the counter to hang up his clippers.

ED

I don't know. Skip it.

EXT. ED'S HOUSE

It is twilight. Ed lifts the latch on the front gate and, cigarette in his mouth, heads up the walk.

Music filters out from the house.

INT. ED'S HOUSE

Ed walks through the living room, hands in his pockets. The music emanates from a radio in the bedroom.

DORIS

Ed?

A track forward reveals Doris sitting at a vanity, doing her hair. Her dress is half zipped at the back.

looking in
mirror

. . . Gimme a zip.

Ed walks over behind her.

ED

Where you going?

DORIS

Me? Us! The party at Nirdlinger's – I told you last week, for the Christmas Push.

ED

Yeah, right.

19

We are close on the zipper as Ed's hand takes the tab, pauses, then lowers it slightly. Her back blooms through the dark fabric of the dress.

He slides the zipper up, and Doris reaches for a perfume atomizer.

> DORIS
> Come on, get ready. It's important.

> ED
> Nah, go ahead. I'm not big on parties.

> DORIS
> Oh, don't be a grump.

SALES FLOOR

It is festooned with streamers.

Ed leans against a wall, one hand dug into a pocket, the other bringing a cigarette to his lips.

Band music plays and Nirdlinger's employees whirl on the dance floor. Bobby-soxed teenagers Lindy-hop and pass palms over their knees.

A thin young man in a sports coat stands next to Ed, watching, his Adam's apple bobbing.

> YOUNG MAN
> Wild, man!

He goes out onto the dance floor. Ed, left by himself, gazes across the floor.

His view, broken by dancers' crosses, shows Big Dave worriedly talking to Doris.

Doris reacts angrily.

Big Dave morosely absorbs the angry words from Doris. He glances up toward Ed and notices his gaze with consternation. He gives Doris a jerk of the head, and she too looks over.

> VOICE
> You in ladies' wear?

The young man with the Adam's apple is back, looking out at the floor, snapping his fingers.

ED

. . . Huh?

YOUNG MAN

Haven't I seen you up in ladies' wear?

ED

I don't work here. My wife does.

YOUNG MAN

Uh-huh. Some beat, huh?

ED

Yeah.

YOUNG MAN

Check out the rack on that broad in the angorra.

ED

Uh-huh.

A hand is laid on Ed's shoulder. It is Big Dave; he leans in to murmur:

DAVE

Ed. Can I talk to you?

BIG DAVE'S OFFICE

Music from the party drifts in only faintly. The office is built into a corner of the sales floor. It is dominated by a large desk. A large window on the far side affords a partial view of the floor.

DAVE

Siddown. Siddown . . .

Ed sits in a leather chair in front of the desk. Dave fumbles nervously on top of the desk for a cigar. He trims the end of the cigar with a short double-bladed knife with a steel grip.

. . . Souveniered it off a Jap in New Guinea.

He hands one cigar to Ed, takes one for himself, then drags up a chair to face Ed's.

. . . I guess you're wondering what Doris was so hot about.

The office is dark, the only illumination coming from the window onto the bright sales floor behind Big Dave. Ed leans forward for Dave to light his cigar.

. . . These're Havanas. Romeo and Juliets. Private stock.

Dave, having lit Ed's cigar, draws nervously on his own.

. . . Ed, I . . .

ED

What is it, Dave?

Dave breaks down, weeping. He buries his face in his hands, the burning cigar in his right hand perilously close to his hair.

DAVE

Ed, I've been weak . . .

His shoulders heave.

. . . I've, uh . . . I've, uh . . . thanks.

Ed has taken Dave's cigar so that he won't burn himself.

. . . I've, uh . . . Oh, Jesus. I've been carrying on with a married woman. Uh, no one you know. And now the, uh – what is it they say? – the – the – the chickens are coming home to roost.

Ed awkwardly holds the two burning cigars.

ED

Uh-huh.

DAVE

Hell, I, I'm not proud of it. But, uh, that's not the worst of it. I got a note. A blackmail note. You know, come across or everybody knows.

ED

Uh-huh.

DAVE

Well, you know what that would do to me.

ED

I guess it would be pretty awkward.

DAVE

Awkward?! Ann'd throw me out on my keister! Hell, it's her
family's store – *her* store. I serve at the indulgence of the goddamn ownership, Ed.

ED

Uh-huh.

DAVE

I only work here! And the lady's husband would know . . .
Oh, Jesus . . .

ED

. . . How much do they want, Dave?

DAVE

$10,000! I don't know what to do, Ed. I don't know what I
can do. Even though I know who the sonofabitch is.

ED

. . . You know . . . who *who* is?

DAVE

The sonofabitch. The blackmailer. It's, uh, it's no one you
know. It's a businessman from Sacramento. A goddamn
pansy, Ed. He tried to rope me into some crackpot scheme; I
heard him out and then told him to go to hell. And the very
next day, the very next day, Ed, I get blackmailed for the
same amount.

ED

Would he . . . it sounds pretty obvious.

DAVE

Well, I guess he don't care that it's obvious.

ED

Mm. How, uh . . . how did he know that –

DAVE

He's staying at the hotel I've gone to with, uh, with the lady
in question. Must've seen us.

Big Dave blows his nose, reaches to take his cigar from Ed.

24

. . . Thanks . . .

He exhales with a long sigh.

. . . Oh, Jesus.

                    ED
. . . Why don't you just pay him, Dave?

                    DAVE
That's my capitalization on the Annex! *My* operation, Ed!
Christ almighty. That's what I was just talking to Doris
about, a way of getting the money from the store that we
could hide from Ann.

                    ED
Mm.

                    DAVE
Embezzling, Ed. From my own goddamn wife!

He gives a tearful chuckle.

. . . Doris, she was pretty hot about that. God bless her. She
doesn't know I'm telling you this – she's mad enough
already. But Jesus, Ed, you're the only one I can talk to. I'm,
I'm sorry I . . . I better get back to the party.

He rises and clears his throat as he rubs the tears from his face.

. . . I look all right?

PULLING ED

*He has left the office to wander through an adjacent room lit only by
spill from the party. It is the music department; pianos and spinets are
arranged across the floor.*

                    ED (V.O.)
In a way I felt bad for Big Dave. I knew the ten grand was
going to pinch him where it hurt . . .

*Ed sits on a piano stool next to a standing ashtray. He takes out a cig-
arette, lights it off his cigar, stubs out the cigar.*

. . . But Doris was two-timing me and I guess, somewhere, that pinched a little too.

His attention is caught by a distant knock of wood. Someone is raising the key-guard on a piano across the room.

The person can be seen only obscurely, from three-quarters behind, through the sales floor's jumble of haphazardly arranged instruments. The person begins to play.

Ed listens. The piece is slow, sweet, almost like a lullaby.

The player, unaware that there is an audience, plays on, and Ed listens, eyes narrowed against the smoke curling past his face.

The piece ends.

voyeuristic

ED

That was pretty.

The player turns, surprised. It is a young woman.

. . . Did you make that up?

YOUNG WOMAN
Oh, no. That was written by Mr Ludwig van Beethoven.

Ed nods recognition of the name.

ED
That was quite something.

YOUNG WOMAN
He wrote some beautiful piano sonatas.

ED
That was something. I'm Ed Crane.

YOUNG WOMAN
I know who you are, Mr Crane.

His look shows surprise.

. . . My father used to take me with him when he got his hair cut. Walter Abundas?

Ed's head tilts back in acknowledgment.

26

. . . I'm Rachel Abundas. Everyone calls me Birdy.

ED

Sorry, I just didn't remember.

BIRDY

Oh, that's all right. You can't be expected to remember every skinny girl who comes in with her dad.

Ed gives a wry smile.

ED

. . . You don't like the music out there?

alone like
him

BIRDY

It's OK, I guess. No, I don't really. I'm not big on music, ordinarily.

A woman calls sharply from offscreen:

VOICE

Ed.

He looks.

Silhouetted in the doorway to the party room is Doris, coat over her arm, purse in hand.

ED'S CAR

Doris and Ed are driving home.

Doris draws heavily on a cigarette, looking flintily out at the road.

> lights flicker over them

DORIS

. . . What a knucklehead.

ED

Who?

DORIS

Dave.

ED

How's that?

DORIS

Ahh . . .

She waves angrily.

. . . Money problems. He's thinking about canceling the Annex.

ED

So?

DORIS

That means I don't run Nirdlinger's!

ED

Mm.

They ride in silence for a beat. Doris shakes her head.

DORIS

. . . What a knucklehead.

STREET

As the car roars past and into the distance.

ANOTHER STREET

It is day. We are looking from inside a parked car toward a hotel

28

entrance. Big Dave emerges from the hotel, gets into a Packard and drives off.

ED (V.O.)

Big Dave did it, though . . .

Ed, sitting in his car, is watching.

. . . I sent a note telling him where to drop the money . . .

HOTEL HALLWAY

Ed emerges from a stairwell and goes to a standing ashtray by the elevator.

ED (V.O.)

. . . and he did. He came across.

Ed reaches into the trash hole in the ashtray column and pulls out a Nirdlinger's bag.

long corridor - shadows
Ed in shadow

He goes back to the stairwell.

ANOTHER FLOOR

camera pans up to next floor thru window.

Ed emerges from the stairwell, goes to a door and knocks.

The door swings open.

CREIGHTON

Yeah, good, how are ya, come in . . .

Ed follows him into the room.

. . . You bring a check?

ED

Cash.

CREIGHTON

Cash?!

He gives Ed a look.

. . . Usually we do this kind of thing with a bank draft. But cash – that's fine – it's all the same in the end – dough's dough, huh?

29

Nervous
- stares at money

ED

Sure.

CREIGHTON

I got the paperwork here. Partnership papers here, they
reflect our agreement: fifty–fifty on the net, I supply professional services, you supply the capital. I'll give you a receipt
on the dough there, huh?

ED

Yeah.

CREIGHTON

Pretty straightforward, but I don't know if you wanna show
this stuff to a lawyer –

ED

It's OK.

CREIGHTON

Yeah, screw 'em, huh? Pay 'em to tangle it up and then you
pay 'em to untangle it, what's the point?

He perspires as he counts the money.

. . . Just a second here, I'll give you a receipt on the, uh . . .
Whoa, Nellie . . . Oh, by the way, we didn't talk about this, I,
uh, I think I'm gonna call the place Tolliver's, after me, you
know, I didn't think you were much interested in, uh –

ED

That'll be fine.

CREIGHTON

Yeah, good. Lemme just, uh . . .

He wipes his brow, finishes counting.

. . . Yeah, that's it. As per our discussion.

ED

Uh-huh.

Creighton hands Ed an executed agreement and a receipt.

CREIGHTON

Well, there it is. Writ large in legal escriture, next step is –

ED

Look, uh . . . Creighton . . .

He gives Creighton a level stare, smoke pluming from the cigarette planted in his mouth.

. . . You're not gonna screw me on this?

CREIGHTON

Screw you – Jesus! Take it to a lawyer! No, I insist! This is *dry* cleaning, this is not some fly-by-night thing here! I must say, I've been an entrepreneur for thirteen years and I've never –

ED

All right.

CREIGHTON

And I've never been asked – Look, you want the dough back? You know who I am! You –

ED

OK.

Creighton mops his brow again.

CREIGHTON

So, uh . . . Tolliver's is OK then?

CAR

Camera on front of car tracking roads

Ed drives with the usual cigarette in his mouth. Doris sits next to him. Rural scenery slips by in the background.

ED (V.O.)

The next day was Saturday. We were going to a reception for Doris's cousin Gina, who'd just married a wop vintner out near Modesto. Doris didn't much feel like going, and I didn't either, but, like she said, we had a Commitment.

Doris gazes stonily out at the road. At length:

DORIS

. . . I hate wops.

Ed gives her a brief glance. Doris glares at him.

. . . What's so damn strange about that?

ED

I didn't say a word.

She looks back out at the road.

DORIS

. . . *You* didn't have to grow up with 'em.

This brings nothing from Ed. Doris shakes her head.

. . . Family. Boy.

BY A BARN

Wops in Sunday clothing greet each other around tables piled with food.

A small child runs up to his mother, yanks on her dress and screams:

CHILD

He's ridin' Garibaldi! Uncle Frankie's ridin' Garibaldi!

Surrounded by cheering children, with a jug of wine slung over his shoulder, Frank is riding an enormous pig. He slaps at the pig's ass with a large straw hat.

ED (V.O.)

That was when she started drinking.

Doris is standing by one of the tables, drinking red wine from a water glass. Ed stands nearby.

A large woman hugs Doris.

WOMAN

How you doin', Doris, you been OK?

DORIS

How're you, Costanza?

WOMAN

Oh, you know, I got my healt'. And how you been, uh . . .

ED

Ed.

WOMAN

Ed. How's a business?

ED

OK.

not sociable

WOMAN
(*to Doris*)

He's a barber, right? It's a good trade. So how come you got
no kids?

PICNIC TABLE

*A group of kids pulls Frank, laughing, by the hand toward a picnic
table set out with pies in a row.*

VOICES

Uncle Frankie's gotta join! Wait for Frankie!

FRANK

No, come on, kids – I just ate lunch!

VOICES

No, no – Uncle Frankie's gotta join!

An old man stands by with a stopwatch:

OLD MAN

Ready . . .

He clicks the timer.

. . . Go!

Frank and the line of children plunge their faces into the line of blueberry pies. Stand By Me?

The other picnickers cheer them on.

ELSEWHERE

Ed and Doris approach the innocent-looking young couple accepting congratulations.

Doris, holding her empty glass, is not a happy drunk:

DORIS

'Gratulations, Gina. It's so goddamn wonderful.

ED

Congratulations, Gina.

DORIS

Life is so goddamn wonderful, you almost won't believe it.

ED

Honey . . .

DORIS

It's just a goddamn bowl a cherries, I'm sure.

Ed tries to lead her away.

ED

Honey . . .

34

Doris calls back over her shoulder:

> DORIS
> Congratulations on your goddamn cherries!

As Ed and Doris recede we hear her petulant:

> . . . Leggo my goddamn elbow.

ELSEWHERE

In long shot we see Frank at the crest of a hill, staggering slowly, painfully, toward a tree. In his right hand he clutches a trophy.

When he reaches the tree he swings his free hand up against it, leans forward, and vomits.

CAR

Late afternoon, driving home.

Ed drives. Doris sits in the front passenger seat, snoring lightly. Frank sits in the back seat hugging his trophy to his chest, eyes closed, murmuring:

> FRANK
> I never wanna see another blueberry pie . . .

Silence.

> . . . I never even wanna hear those words.

Doris moans.

More silence.

> . . . Don't say those words, Ed.

EXT. BUNGALOW — the bannion house

It is twilight. Ed's coupe is parked in the driveway. He is just rounding the back of the car to open the passenger-side door. He pulls Doris from the car, half asleep, half drunk.

INT. BUNGALOW

The door swings open and Ed stumbles in supporting Doris, who has one arm draped around his neck. He helps her into the bedroom and eases her onto the bed. ~~Light through window~~

He sits on the edge of the bed and looks down at her. ~~dappled~~

Shadows from branches just outside wave across her face. She is breathing through her open mouth; her face is moist with perspiration.

> ED (V.O.)
> I'd met Doris blind on a double-date with a loudmouthed buddy of mine who was seeing a friend of hers from work. We went to a movie; Doris had a flask; we killed it. She could put it away. At the end of the night she said she liked it I didn't talk much. A couple weeks later she suggested –

A harsh jangle from the telephone. Doris moans but does not wake; Ed rises and goes to the living room and picks up the phone.

> ED
> Yeah.

> VOICE
> Ed, it's Big Dave. I gotta talk to you.

> ED
> What – now?

> DAVE
> Please, Ed.

> ED
> But it's . . .

> DAVE
> Please, Ed.

Ed sighs.

> ED
> Your place?

> DAVE
> I'm at Nirdlinger's. Let yourself in.

ED

OK.

He hangs up.

He nudges Doris.

. . . Honey.

She murmurs.

. . . Honey.

She rolls away and burrows into a pillow.

Ed opens her purse and pokes through it.

NIRDLINGER'S *LA shot over store - neon sign + light cast over door*

We are looking over Ed's shoulder as he hesitantly swings open a door.

It reveals Big Dave's office, quiet and rather dark. *light from desk lamp*

A down-facing banker's lamp on the desk illuminates Big Dave's hands on the desktop. *→ cant see face.*

ED

. . . Dave?

DAVE

Come on in.

Ed enters, sits.

An awkward silence.

ED

. . . What's the problem, Big Dave?

Another silence.

DAVE

. . . I'm ruined.

His hands writhe on the desktop.

. . . It ruined me. This money. No annex. I'm all shot to hell.

ED

So you paid the guy?

Big Dave stares without speaking.

After a long beat:

DAVE

. . . What kind of man *are* you?

ED

. . . Huh?

DAVE

What kind of man *are* you?

ED

Big Dave –

DAVE

I'd understand if you'd walked in here. Socked me in the nose. Whatever. I deserved it.

ED

I, uh . . .

music deep, looming strings

I'm not proud of what I did. But *you.*

No one talks.

Big Dave sighs.

camera moving
in on them

...Yeah, I paid up. As you well know. And then I went and found the pansy.

shot for
shot

He looks at Ed.

... Got nothin' to say, huh? Yeah, well, you already know the story. I didn't, I hadda beat it out of the pansy. *Your* money.

No response.

... What kind of man *are* you?

Big Dave rises.

... Well.

He crosses around the desk and adds, sadly:

... I'm all shot to hell.

Ed starts to rise, but Big Dave is already looming over him. Big Dave bear-hugs him and then spins him into a wall.

Ed hits the wall and bounces off, back into Big Dave. Big Dave wallops him in the stomach. Ed doubles over.

... What kind of man *are* you?

Big Dave hurls him against the desk, then slams his face against the desktop. Ed's hands scrabble at the top of the desk as Big Dave grabs him by the neck and lifts. He slams him face-first into the window between the office and the dark sales floor.

Ed twists around, the back of his head now pressed against the glass. Big Dave's hands lock around his throat.

Big Dave sweats and strains.

A crack shoots up the pane of glass.

Ed's hand sweeps up and plunges something into Big Dave's neck.

Big Dave grunts and turns away, gurgling. His hands go up to his throat.

Ed watches. He is holding Big Dave's cigar trimmer.

Big Dave takes a couple of deliberate steps backward, his head twisted away.

He falls back, tripped up by a chair, which spins him face-down onto the floor.

Big Dave crawls away face-down across the floor, on his knees but with his hands still at his throat. His face and knees awkwardly support his weight as if he were pushing something across the floor with his nose.

He reaches a corner but still pushes forward, wedging himself in, legs still scraping away as if to push himself through the wall. Blood is pooling out from under him.

Big Dave's legs are still working. His gurgling continues.

Ed watches.

Big Dave's legs start to move furiously. They convulse. His whole body shakes as he goes into shock.

Ed watches.

Big Dave stops shaking. He remains wedged awkwardly into the corner, face-down. He is still.

The room is very quiet.

Ed looks down at his hands.

He walks across the room, pushes the door open and walks across the darkened sales floor.

EXT. STORE

Ed walks to his car. He does not look about, is not particularly furtive. He gets into the car. He starts the ignition.

EXT. HOUSE

He pulls up, sits motionless for a beat. Gradually, something draws his attention; he cocks his head and looks up through the windshield.

A branch creaks and sways in the breeze.

INT. HOUSE

Ed gets into bed next to Doris. He stares at the ceiling. Wind rustles outside.

The shadow of a branch on the ceiling nods in time with the wind.

He looks at Doris.

Her face is still lightly sheened with sweat but her mouth is closed now, her breathing more peaceful. The leafy shadows play over her face.

> ED (V.O.)
> . . . It was only a couple of weeks after we met that Doris suggested getting married. I said, Don't you wanna get to know me more? She said, Why, does it get better? She looked at me like I was a dope, which I've never really minded from her. And she had a point, I guess. We knew each other as well then as now . . .

He is gazing at her.

> . . . Anyway, well enough.

Sound and image fade.

BARBERSHOP

The next day.

Ed cuts hair, a cigarette between his lips.

> FRANK
> Holy-moly, do I got a headache.

Frank is giving a haircut as well.

> . . . How you today, Ed?

> ED
> OK.

FRANK

You don't got a headache?

ED

. . . Nah.

FRANK

Damn, I got a headache to beat the band.

LATER

Ed sits in his chair, hands folded in his lap, head tilted back, eyes closed.

We hold on Ed as we hear a clipper buzzing and Frank talking to someone in his chair:

FRANK

Ya can't pump it. Did ya pump it? That'll just flood it.

CUSTOMER

Ya gotta pump it. Ya can't just hold it down. *That*'ll flood it.

FRANK

You crazy? You pumped it?

CUSTOMER

Well, ya can't hold it down.

There is the jingle of the door bell. Ed opens his eyes.

Two men in fedoras are entering. detectives

Ed starts to rise.

MAN I

Ed Crane?

ED

Right.

MAN I

Come on outside.

ED

Sure.

OUTSIDE

The two men are staring at the sidewalk, smoking, hesitant to speak.
One of them finally comes up with an icebreaker:

MAN 2

. . . So you're a barber, huh?

ED

That's right.

MAN I

I'm Officer Persky. This is Krebs.

Ed nods toward their car:

ED

. . . We goin'?

KREBS

Huh? No.

Beat.

PERSKY

. . . Cigarette?

Ed holds up one hand with its smoking cigarette.

Right. Uh . . . Pete's got some news for you.

His partner gives Persky a dirty look.

KREBS

. . . Look, pal, it's a tough break, but, uh . . . well damnit,
your wife's been pinched.

PERSKY

They sent us around to tell ya.

ED

Huh?

KREBS

They sent us to tell ya. We pulled the detail.

43

ED

My *wife?*

PERSKY

Yeah, uh, they brung her to the county jail, uh . . .

KREBS

Homicide.

PERSKY

Well, embezzlement. And homicide. A guy named David
Brewster. He's, uh . . . He's the decedant.

ED

I don't understand.

KREBS

He's the dead guy.

Ed stares at him.

PERSKY

. . . Yeah, it's a tough break.

KREBS

Visiting ends at five. Too late today. You can see her tomorrow.

PERSKY

Sorry, pal. They sent us to tell ya.

He shakes his head.

. . . Crap detail.

RESIDENTIAL STREET

*It is evening. Ed is pulling up to a house on a tree-lined street similar to
his own. He gets out of his car and goes up the walk, and a man sitting
on the porch swing holds up a hand of greeting.*

MAN

'Lo, Ed.

ED

Hello, Walter.

44

He steps up to the porch.

The man is holding a tumbler of whiskey and ice that clinks as the swing moves. His skin glistens with drinker's sweat, and he has the slightly expansive manner of someone who's put at least a couple away.

> WALTER

Have a seat.

Ed glances around but the swing is the only seat. He sits next to Walter.

> ED

Thanks. Thanks for seeing me, at home.

> WALTER

Oh, hell. Drink?

> ED

No thanks.

> WALTER

Sure you don't need one?

> ED

I'm fine.

> WALTER

OK. Boy. Jesus!

> ED

Yeah. What do I, uh . . .

> WALTER

Well, of course, I, uh, it's out of my league, criminal stuff. I do, uh, probate, real estate, title search, uh . . . I'd be absolutely worthless, something like this. Absolutely worthless.

He belches.

'Scuse me, just finished dinner. Um. Frankly, Doris'd be better off with the county defender.

> ED

He a good man?

sound of crickets

WALTER

Bert's OK, sure, he's a good man. I won't kid you though, Ed,
nobody around here has any experience with this kind of, er . . .
And I hear they're bringing a prosecutor up from Sacramento.
Capital offense. Taking it seriously . . . Hmm . . .

ED

So –

WALTER

Taking it seriously.

ED

So, who should I –

The front door opens and someone speaks through the screen:

VOICE

You want any coffee, Dad?

Ed looks around at the voice.

Oh, hello, Mr Crane.

She steps out: it is Birdy Abundas.

dappled shadows
across her

Ed rises, and they awkwardly shake hands.

ED

Hello, Rachel.

BIRDY

I'm so sorry . . . I was sorry to hear.

ED

Yeah. Thanks.

WALTER

Coffee, Ed?

ED

I'm fine. Thanks.

WALTER

No thanks, honey.

46

BIRDY

OK. Nice to see you, Mr Crane.

They watch her go back in.

WALTER

Damnit! She's a good kid.

Ed nods.

A beat.

ED

. . . So, uh, who should I –

WALTER

Well, there's Lloyd Garroway in San Francisco. Probity –
you know, no one ever said anything iffy about Lloyd Garroway. Conservative. Jury might like that. Might like that
here.

He takes a sip of his drink.

. . . Probity.

ED

Uh-huh. Is he the best then, for, uh . . .

WALTER

Well, the best, the money-is-no-object best, for a criminal
case, any lawyer would tell you Freddy Riedenschneider. Out
of Sacramento. 'Course, I don't know how you're fixed for
money.

ED

Uh-huh. He's the, uh . . .

WALTER

Yeah, the best.

He sniffs.

. . . Yeah, Riedenschneider. Wish I could tell you more. Hell,
I wish I could handle it myself. But I'd be absolutely worthless for this kind of thing.

47

He takes a musing sip.

    . . . Criminal matter? Freddy Riedenschneider.

He thinks.

    . . . No question about it.

ED AT A TABLE

It is a long table with chairs stretching down both sides, one side for prisoners, the other for visitors. The room is empty except for a guard and an elderly woman who sits across from a younger woman at the far end of the table. The younger woman, in a prison smock, is wailing. The elderly woman is holding her hand.

Ed sits across from an empty chair, clutching a flower-printed toiletries kit. There are echoing voices suggesting large spaces outside the room.

He sits and waits.

Approaching footsteps.

The door opens. A large prison matron steps aside to let Doris enter.

Doris looks lost in a prison-issue jumper that is too big for her. Her hair is uncurled and bedraggled. Not only is she not made-up, she has a couple of bruises and a cut on her lip.

As Ed stands, she gives a hollow look around. trailing smoke over her face

> ED
> Honey . . . I brought your make-up.

She looks at him.

> DORIS
> Honey.

> ED
> How are you?

She shrugs.

> DORIS
> I don't know what's going on. I –

48

ED

What happened to you?

She shakes her head.

DORIS

. . . I don't know what happened to Big Dave. I know some of it. Irregularities in my books, they said. Can I explain it.

ED

You don't have to –

DORIS

I helped him cook the books, Ed. I did do that.

ED

You don't have to tell them anything. We're getting you a lawyer.

Doris doesn't seem to be listening. She sighs:

DORIS

I know all about that. But I don't know how much to tell them.

ED

Don't tell 'em anything. We're getting you Freddy Rieden-schneider.

Doris finally looks at him.

DORIS

Should I . . . should I tell you why?

ED

You don't have to tell me anything.

Her gaze drifts away again. She notices the sobbing woman.

DORIS

Jesus Christ.

Doris looks around and laughs.

. . . My books used to be perfect. Anyone could open them up, make sense of the whole goddamn store.

Honey . . .

I knew we'd pay for it.

BARBERSHOP

Ed sits in a waiting-customer chair, wearing his smock. Frank paces in front of him. He smacks a fist into his palm.

FRANK

This is what family is for, Ed! This is when ya come together!

ED

Yeah.

FRANK

Close ranks! Goddamnit! Those sons of bitches!

ED

Frank, uh, you know I'll try to contribute, but, uh – Freddy Riedenschneider –

FRANK

I don't care what it costs! This is when ya come together!

ED

That's very generous.

FRANK

The hell with it, Eddie!

BANK

Ed and Frank sit waiting on a bench in the high-vaulted lobby. Frank looks uncomfortable in an ill-fitting suit. As they wait, he looks nervously about.

In a hushed voice:

FRANK

They're just people like you and me, Ed. Remember that.

ED

Uh-huh.

FRANK

Just people. They gotta put up the big front so that people will trust them with their money. This is why the big lobby, Ed. But they put their pants on one leg at a time. Just like you and me.

ED

Uh-huh.

FRANK

They too use the toilet, Ed. In spite of appearances. And their money will be secured by the barbershop. A rock. A *rock*, the barbershop. I mean, how long has *this* place been here?

A door opens. A conservatively dressed man of late middle age emerges.

MAN

Mr Raffo?

Frank hops to his feet.

FRANK

Yes, sir.

MAN

Could you come with me please?

FRANK

Sure. Can Ed come too?

The man looks dubiously at Ed.

MAN

Mr . . .?

ED

Crane. Ed Crane.

MAN

You also have an interest in the securing property?

He's a barber.

MAN

Ah.

FRANK

Second chair.

MAN

Not an owner.

FRANK

No, he's family, he's my brother-in-law.

MAN

Ah-hah. It would be best if he waited here.

He goes to the glass-paned doorway to his office, Frank trailing deject-
edly behind. They enter, the door closes, and we hear their muffled
voices from inside, the sense of the words lost. ꞁꞁꞁꞁꞁ ꞁꞁꞁꞁꞁꞁꞁ

Ed sits and watches the two men perform their pantomime of business:
Frank nervously reads documents with one hand cupped to his fore-
head for concentration; the banker passes successive documents across
his desk with a word of explanation for each as Frank signs.

Ed takes out a cigarette and lights it, watching impassively.

ED (V.O.)

The barbershop. Doris and Frank's father had worked thirty
years to own it free and clear. Now it got signed over to the
bank, and the bank signed some money over to Frank, and
Frank signed the money over . . .

TRACKING POINT OF VIEW

It is midday. We are tracking along the sidewalk toward a long cream-
colored Packard parked at the curb. A couple of kids have stopped to
peer into the car's windows; the car is no doubt the fanciest in town.

ED (V.O.)

. . . to Freddy Riedenschneider, who got into town two days
later . . .

Ed, coming up the sidewalk, looks up at the storefront: a restaurant with a large window with a plush red drape that obscures the interior. Gilt lettering on the window spells out DAVINCI'S.

. . . and told me to meet him at DaVinci's for lunch.

TRACKING POINT OF VIEW

Inside the restaurant. We are tracking toward a table whose lone occupant sits with his back to us holding open a menu as he orders from a facing waitress:

> MAN
> . . . not fried, poached. Three of 'em for two minutes. A strip steak medium rare, flapjacks, potatoes, tomato juice, and plenty of hot coffee.

He flips the menu over.

. . . Do you have prairie oysters?

> WAITRESS
> No, sir.

> MAN
> Then bring me a fruit cocktail while I wait.

He looks up at Ed.

. . . You're Crane?

> ED
> Yeah –

> MAN
> Barber, right? I'm Freddy Riedenschneider. Hungry? They tell me the chow's OK here. I made some inquiries.

> ED
> No thanks, I –

The waitress sets a fruit cocktail in front of Riedenschneider.

> RIEDENSCHNEIDER
> Look, I don't wanna waste your time so I'll eat while we talk. Ya mind? *You* don't mind. So while I'm in town I'll be stay-

ing at the Hotel Metropole, the Turandot Suite. Yeah, it's goofy, the suites're named after operas; room's OK though, I poked around. I'm having 'em hold it for me on account of I'll be back and forth. In addition to my retainer, you're paying hotel, living expenses, secretarial, private eye if we need to make inquiries, headshrinker should we go that way. We'll talk about appeals if, as and when. For right now, has she confessed?

ED

No. Of course not. She didn't do it.

RIEDENSCHNEIDER

Good! That helps. Not that she didn't do it, that she didn't confess. Of course, there's ways to deal with a confession, but that's good! – one less thing to think about. Now. Interview. I'm seeing her tomorrow. You should be there. Three o'clock. One more thing: you keep your mouth shut. I get the lay of the land, *I* tell *you* what to say. No talking out of school. What's out of school? Everything's out of school. I do the talking; you keep your trap shut. I'm an attorney, you're a barber; you don't know anything. Understood?

ED

. . . OK.

RIEDENSCHNEIDER

Good! Any questions give me a ring – Turandot suite; if I'm out leave a message. You sure you don't want anything? No?

He points a finger at Ed.

. . . You're OK, pal. You're OK, she's OK. Everything's gonna be hunky-dory.

The waitress puts down a plate of steak and eggs.

. . . And the flapjacks, honey.

DRIVING POINT OF VIEW

We are looking at pedestrians on the sidewalk through the windshield of a moving car.

54

ED (V.O.)

All going about their business. It seemed like I knew a secret
– a bigger one even than what had really happened to Big
Dave, something none of them knew . . .

On Ed, driving.

. . . Like I had made it to the outside, somehow, and they
were all still struggling, way down below.

ED IN BED

Arms folded behind his head, staring at the ceiling.

On the ceiling is the moving shadow of a tree limb.

A distant, muffled knock.

Ed turns his head.

FRONT DOOR

Ed opens it as he finishes cinching a bathrobe.

*The woman waiting on the front porch is dressed in black: a black dress
and a black veiled hat that is too big for her bird-like frame.*

Wind rustles in the trees behind her.

She stares at Ed.

ED

Ann.

For the first time, we hear her speak, in a low, tremulous voice:

ANN

Hello, Ed.

ED

Ann. Will you come in?

She shakes her head.

ANN

. . . No. No, it's very late.

Ed nods.

After an uncomfortable beat, through which she continues to stare:

> ED
>
> . . . I'm so sorry about your loss.

looming string music [handwritten]

> ANN
>
> Yes. Thank you.

> ED
>
> Of course, you know, Doris had nothing to do with it. Nothing at all.

She lays a black-gloved hand on his arm.

> ANN
>
> Oh, I know. Don't worry, Ed. I came to tell you . . .

> ED
>
> Yes, Ann?

> ANN
>
> And you should tell Doris . . .

She falls silent. The trees behind her rustle.

She gives a wary look back. Then, confidingly, to Ed:

sound of wind howling [handwritten]

> . . . You know how Big Dave loved camping. And the out-of-doors.

Ed is puzzled:

> ED
>
> Yes?

> ANN
>
> We went camping last summer. In Eugene, Oregon. *Outside* of Eugene, Ed.

She gives him a searching look, hoping, it seems, that he will find this significant.

> ED
>
> . . . Yes?

ANN

At night, there were lights – we both saw them. We never told anyone, outside of our official report.

ED

Ann –

ANN

A spacecraft. I saw the creatures. They led Big Dave onto the craft. He never told anyone what they did, outside of his report. Of course he told *me*. No one else.

ED

Ann –

ANN

The government knows. I cannot repeat it to you. But this thing goes deep, Ed. This was not your wife. It goes deep, and involves the government. There is a great deal of fear. You know how certain circles would find it – the knowledge – a threat. They try to limit it, and –

ED

Ann, will you come in, sit down, maybe have a drink?

ANN

Sometimes knowledge is a curse, Ed. After this happened,
things changed. Big Dave . . . he never touched me again.

Ed says nothing.

She touches his arm.

. . . Tell Doris not to worry. I know it wasn't her. Perhaps this
will bring it out, finally. Perhaps now it will all come out.

She turns and heads down the walk.

*Her high-heeled footsteps echo on the walk, then the sidewalk, then are
lost in the rustle of leaves.*

Ed watches her go: a small black figure, growing smaller.

PRISON MEETING ROOM

*It is an unadorned room with a simple wooden table and chairs. One
high window lets in a shaft of sunlight.*

*Ed and Doris sit at the table; Freddy Riedenschneider stands to one
side staring up at the high window, hands dug into his pockets.*

All three are motionless for a long beat. Finally:

RIEDENSCHNEIDER

. . . It stinks.

DORIS

But it's true.

RIEDENSCHNEIDER

I don't care it's true, it's not true; it stinks. You say he was
being blackmailed; by who? You don't know. For having an
affair; with who? You don't know. Did anyone else know
about it? Probably not; you don't know.

ED

I knew about it. Big Dave told me about it, and the spot he
was putting himself in by getting the money.

RIEDENSCHNEIDER

Terrific. Your husband backs you up. That's terrific.

58

He starts pacing.

. . . You've gotta give me something to work with. Freddy Riedenschneider is good, but he's not a magician. He can't just wave his little wand in the air and make a plausible defense materialize. Look. Look at what the other side is gonna run at us. They got the company books, prepared by you – *cooked* by you – that's Motive. They got a murder scene *you* had access to. That's Opportunity. They got that little trimmer thing he was stabbed in the throat with – a *dame's* weapon –

ED

It was Big Dave's.

RIEDENSCHNEIDER

– don't interrupt me – that's Means. They got a fine upstanding pillar of the business community as a victim, and then they got *you*, a disgruntled number-juggling underling who on the day in question was drunk as a skunk and whose alibi for the time in question is being passed out at home, alone.

ED

I was with her.

Riedenschneider gives him a hard look.

RIEDENSCHNEIDER

. . . Like I say, it stinks.

Another long pause.

ED

. . . I killed him.

Riedenschneider eyes him. Wheels start turning.

RIEDENSCHNEIDER

OK, we forget the blackmail. *You* killed him. How come?

ED

He and Doris . . . were having an affair.

Doris eyes him. His manner does not reveal anything.

59

RIEDENSCHNEIDER
...id you know?

ED
I . . ., knew. A husband knows.

Riedenschneider rolls his eyes.

RIEDENSCHNEIDER
Will anyone else say they knew?

ED
I don't know. I don't think so.

RIEDENSCHNEIDER
How did you get into the store?

ED
I took Doris's keys.

RIEDENSCHNEIDER
Will anyone say they saw you there? On your way there? In there? On your way back?

ED
. . . I don't think so.

RIEDENSCHNEIDER
Will anyone corroborate any goddamn part of your story at all?

Ed returns Riedenschneider's stare. Riedenschneider resumes pacing.

. . . Come on, people. You can't help each other like that. Let's be realistic now. Let's look at our options. Well, frankly, I don't *see* any options.

A nod of the head indicates Doris:

. . . I cannot present Story A.

Another nod indicates Ed:

. . . I cannot present Story B. I could plead you for a nutcase but you look too composed. I could offer a guilty plea and in return they don't give you the juice, but I don't think you want to spend the rest of your life in Chino and I know you didn't hire Freddy Riedenschneider to hold your hand at a sentencing hearing. Hell, you could've gotten Lloyd Garroway for that. No, we're not giving up yet; you hired Freddy Riedenschneider, it means you're *not* throwing in the towel. I litigate, I don't capitulate. All right, no options, we gotta think. All right, we go back to the blackmail thing. It titillates, it's open-ended . . .

His pacing becomes more animated.

. . . And it makes *him* the bad guy – ya dig around, ya never know, something unsavory from his past, he approaches you to help with the money, it's too late, his past comes back to haunt him, who's to say . . .

He is heading for the door.

. . . Yeah. OK. Forget the jealous husband thing, that's silly; we're going with the blackmail. I'll be in touch.

The door slams.

HOTEL LOBBY

The camera drifts in toward the reception desk. Ed talks to the clerk behind the desk, but the scene plays silently; we hear only Ed's narration.

ED (V.O.)
Of course, there was *one* person who could confirm Doris's story, or plenty of it: the dry-cleaning pansy . . .

The desk clerk is shaking his head.

. . . But he'd left the hotel, skipped out on his bill . . .

[handwritten: become detective – trying to find him]

HALLWAY

It is a rooming-house hallway. A stern middle-aged woman is on the hall telephone. This too plays silently under the narration.

ED (V.O.)
He'd also disappeared from the residence he gave me . . .

ED'S LIVING ROOM

We are drifting in toward Ed, who nods at the telephone and then cradles it. He stares down at the business card he holds.

ED (V.O.)

. . . owing two months' rent. How could I have been so stupid. Handing over $10,000. For a piece of paper. And the man gone . . . like a ghost . . .

PULLING BACK FROM ED

In a different living room. He sits on a sofa, hands clasped behind his head, listening. For the first time, as the voice-over continues, we hear atmosphere from the scene: piano music.

ED (V.O.)

. . . disappeared into thin air, vaporized, like the Nips at Nagasaki. Gone now. All gone. The money gone. Big Dave gone. Doris going. How could I have been so stupid?

The continuing pull-back reveals Walter Abundas on a nearby chair, also listening as Birdy plays.

Walter holds a drink in one hand; he is nodding; his eyelids droop. As the piano piece reaches its mournful conclusion his chin alights on his chest, his eyelids tremble closed, and he starts lightly to snore.

BARBERSHOP

The distinctive buzz of electric hairclippers bangs in at the cut. Ed and Frank stand behind their respective chairs, administering haircuts.

The customer in Ed's chair is in white shirtsleeves that do not hide rolls of fat. He has a hot towel over his face that does not slow his speech, although it does muffle it to some extent:

CUSTOMER

She makes this stuff, she calls it gatto, it's got egg in there, it's got sugar, it's got – it's cake, basically, except she calls it gatto. Like if you don't call it cake maybe you won't put on any weight, like I need to eat gatto, you know what I'm saying? This stuff, if I've had a square meal, I've had my steak and potatoes, I can just have another cup of coffee afterward, I won't ask for the dessert if it's not there . . .

His voice turns into a drone under the narration.

                    ED (V.O.)
Sooner or later everyone needs a haircut . . .

                    CUSTOMER
Got the recipe from a magazine, woman's magazine . . .

                    ED (V.O.)
We were working for the bank now. We kept cutting the hair, trying to stay afloat, make the payments, tread the water, day by day, day by day . . .

CRANE DOWN

Inside a courtroom we boom down toward the defendant's table, the fat customer's drone turning into the drone of the bailiff reading an indictment. Doris stands next to Freddy Riedenschneider.

                    ED (V.O.)
Most people think someone's accused of a crime, they haul 'em in and bring 'em to trial, but it's not like that, it's

not that fast. The wheels of justice turn slow . . .

BAILIFF

. . . did willfully and with malice aforethought take the life of
one David Allen Brewster, a human being . . .

ED (V.O.)

They have the arraignment, and then the indictment, and
they entertain motions to dismiss, and postpone, and change
the venue, and alter this and that and the other. They
empanel a jury, which brings more motions, and they set a
trial date and then change the date, and then often as not
they'll change it again.

BAILIFF

What say you to these charges?

*Our boom down has ended close on Doris. We hear Freddy Rieden-
schneider, off:*

RIEDENSCHNEIDER

We plead not guilty, your honor.

BARBERSHOP

Booming down toward the fat man.

ED (V.O.)

And through all of it we cut the hair.

CUSTOMER

I say, Honey, if you're gonna make cobbler, make a little bit
of cobbler, don't put a whole pan in front of me and tell me
it's not gonna be any good when it's cold . . .

OPERA SINGERS

*We are panning photographic portraits of opera singers in character,
wearing the wardrobe of different eras, armies, dukedoms, and boudoirs,
and displaying the heights and depths of various emotions, their mouths
stretched wide in song. We pan off the pictures to discover that we are in
a hotel room, floating in toward a bed on which Freddy Riedenschneider, a mask over his eyes, slumbers.*

ED (V.O.)

. . . Meantime, Freddy Riedenschneider slept at the Metropole . . .

RESTAURANT

Tracking in toward Freddy Riedenschneider, who sits twirling spaghetti with a fork against a spoon.

ED (V.O.)

. . . and shoveled it in at DaVinci's.

LATERAL TRACK

From inside a car. Pedestrians bustle along a sidewalk. Among them scurries a weedy little man who has one hand clamped to the crown of his hat to keep it in place in a stiff wind.

ED (V.O.)

He'd brought in a private investigator from Sacramento . . .

LATERAL TRACK

Moving the opposite way. A different day, but again a crowd moves along the sidewalk, and among them the little man scuttles in the opposite direction, hand still raised to his hat, his forearm and the tilt of his head largely obscuring his face.

ED (V.O.)

. . . to nose around into Big Dave's past.

PUSHING IN TO ED

In the Abundas living room again, again listening to Birdy at the piano, but now the two of them are alone.

ED (V.O.)

I found myself more and more going over to the Abundas's. It was a routine we fell into, most every evening. I even went when Walter was away on his research trips. He was a genealogist, had traced back his side of the family seven generations, his late wife's, eight. It seemed like a screwy hobby. But then maybe all hobbies are. Maybe Walter found something

library scene

65

there, in the old county courthouses, hospital file rooms, city archives, property rolls, registries, something maybe like what I found listening to Birdy play. Some kind of escape. Some kind of peace . . .

The piano music ends in a sustain which begins to fade, but then is snapped by a sharp clang.

PRISON DOOR SWINGS OPEN

We are pushing into the high-windowed prison meeting room. None of its three occupants is moving.

The tableau consists of Doris staring down at the table; the private investigator sitting on a straightbacked chair tipped back against a wall, his arms folded across his chest, his fedora pushed back on his head, a toothpick clamped between his teeth; and Freddy Riedenschneider, standing, hands clasped behind his back, gazing with a distant smile up into the shaft of light that slants through the high window.

A warder shuts the door behind Ed.

Doris and the private investigator turn to note his entrance; Riedenschneider does not.

Ed pulls out a chair across from Doris, clasps his hands on top of hers.

ED

'Lo, honey.

She looks at his hands on top of hers.

A long beat.

Still gazing up into the shaft of light, Freddy Riedenschneider announces:

RIEDENSCHNEIDER

. . . They got this guy, in Germany. Fritz something-or-other. Or is it. Maybe it's Werner. Anyway, he's got this theory, you wanna test something, you know, scientifically – how the planets go round the sun, what sunspots are made of, why the water comes out of the tap – well, you gotta look at it. But sometimes, you look at it, your looking *changes* it. Ya can't know the reality of what happened, or what *would*'ve happened if you hadden a stuck in your own goddamn schnozz. So there *is* no 'what happened.' Not in any sense that we can grasp with our puny minds. Because our minds . . . our minds get in the way. Looking at something changes it. They call it the 'Uncertainty Principle.' Sure, it sounds screwy, but even Einstein says the guy's on to something.

His gaze up at the window breaks. He strolls around the room, still smiling.

. . . Science. Perception. Reality. Doubt . . .

He stops to examine a bur on his fingernail.

. . . Reasonable doubt. I'm sayin', sometimes, the more you look, the less you really know. It's a fact. A proved fact. In a way, it's the only fact there is. This heinie even wrote it out in numbers.

He looks up at the private detective.

. . . Burns?

With a slight weight shift, Burns tips his chair so that its front legs slap down onto the floor. He fishes a small notebook from an inside pocket.

His boredom is profound; his only concession to performance is to move the toothpick from one side of his mouth to the other where, perhaps, it will less inhibit speech.

BURNS
Subject: David Allen Brewster. Born: Cincinatti, 1911. Father: insurance salesman; mother: homemaker. One year Case Western University on football scholarship. Flunks out. 1931: retail appliance salesman in Barnhoff's department store, Cincinatti. 1933: meets Ann Nirdlinger, married later that year, moves here. 1935: arrested on an assault complaint; complainant, an organizer for the ILGWU, has a broken nose, couple a ribs, wife's family intercedes, some kind of settlement, charges dropped. 1936: another assault beef, bar altercation –

RIEDENSCHNEIDER
Yeah, yeah, couple of fistfights. Go to his service record.

Burns looks at him sourly. He flips a couple of pages.

> BURNS
> ... Inducted March 15, 1942, assigned to fifth fleet US Navy, petty officer first class, serves in clerical capacity in US naval shipyards in San Diego, one fistfight broken up by MPs, no court martial, honorable discharge May 8, 1945. Since then he's been clean.

Riedenschneider nods, smiling.

> RIEDENSCHNEIDER
> ... Thank you, Burns, get lost.

Burns pockets his notebook, adjusts his hat, jams his hands into his pockets, and ambles out of the room.

The slam of the door leaves quiet.

At length:

> ED
> ... So?

Riedenschneider's fixed smile now fades.

> RIEDENSCHNEIDER
> So? *So?!* This could be your dolly's ticket out of the death-house, so!

Ed and Doris look at each other.

> ED
> ... I don't get it.

> RIEDENSCHNEIDER
> Look, chum, this is a guy, from what I understand, told everybody he was a war hero, right? Island hopping, practically liberated the Pacific all by himself with a knife in one hand and a gun in the other and twenty yards of Jap guts between his teeth.

> ED
> Yeah.

RIEDENSCHNEIDER

And now it turns out this dope spent the war sitting on his
ass in some boatyard in San Diego. You asked for blackmail,
let me give you blackmail: Mr Hale-Fellow-Well-Met, about
to open his own business here, has been lying to everybody
in this town for the last four years, probably including half
the people sitting on that jury. Well, it finally caught up with
him – these dopes, it always does; someone threatened to
spill it. Somebody knew his dirty little secret, just like your
wife says. They called, they demanded money . . .

He is looking at Doris.

. . . Did Big Dave mention that it was something about his
war service? I don't know, I wasn't there, *you'll* have to tell *us*.
Maybe he specified, maybe he didn't; I'm not putting words
in your mouth; the point is that this liar, this cynical manipu-
lator, this man who through his lies sneered and belittled the
sacrifice and heroism of all our boys who *did* serve and bleed
and puke and die on foreign shores, and who made a fool out
of this entire town, turns to *you* to help him out of his jam.
Fat-assed sonofabitch!

ED

So . . . who . . . who actually –

RIEDENSCHNEIDER

Who? *Who?!* I don't know who! But the point is that if Mr
Prosecutor over there had devoted half the time he's spent
persecuting *this* woman to even the most cursory investiga-
tion of this schmoe's past, then we might *know* who! But we
can't *know* what really happened! Because of Fritz, or
Werner, or whatever the hell his name is! And because Mr
Prosecutor is *also* a lazy fat-assed sonofabitch who decided
it's easier to victimize your wife! Because it's easier *not* to
look! Because the more you look, the less you know! But the
beauty of it is, we don't *gotta* know! We just gotta show that,
goddamnit, *they* don't know. Reasonable doubt. Science. The
atom. *You* explain it to me. Go ahead. Try.

He chuckles as he heads for the door.

. . . Yeah, Freddy Riedenschneider sees daylight. We got a real shot at this, folks. Let's not get cocky.

The door shuts behind him.

Doris stares down at the table, as at the head of the scene.

A silent beat; a smile starts to tug at the corners of her mouth.

ED

Honey . . .?

The smile twitches, and then stays. Doris starts to laugh. Ed frowns.

. . . Honey?

Her laughter builds, almost to hysteria. Finally it subsides and, still staring at the tabletop and smiling, she shakes her head:

DORIS

What a dope.

ABUNDAS LIVING ROOM

Ed sits listening as Birdy plays. She talks, after a moment, her eyes on the sheet music:

BIRDY

He was deaf when he wrote this.

ED

Who?

BIRDY

Beethoven. He created it, and yet he never actually heard it. I suppose he heard it all in his head, somehow.

Over her continued playing:

ED (V.O.)

So maybe Riedenschneider could get Doris off. Maybe it would all work out. And I thought – I hoped – that maybe there was a way out for me as well . . .

A SIGN

The cardboard sign on an easel says COME ONE, COME ALL/
PETALUMA HIGH SCHOOL TALENT SHOW/WEDNESDAY APRIL 29,
1949, 8:00 P.M.

ED (V.O.)

 The girl had talent, anyone could see that. And *she* wasn't
some fly-by-nighter, she was just a good clean kid . . .

SCHOOL GYMNASIUM

*A young man holding a saxophone is just leaving the makeshift stage
to a smattering of applause. Birdy walks out to the baby grand that
has been set out center stage.*

ED (V.O.)

. . . If she was going to have a career she'd need a responsible
adult looking out for her . . .

*We track up the rows of folding chairs that have been set out on the
gym floor for the audience of students and parents, many of whom fan
themselves with programs. We come to rest on Ed.*

. . . some kind of . . . manager. She'd have contracts to look

at, be going out on tours, playing on the radio maybe. I could help her sort through all of that, without charging her an arm and a leg, just enough to get by . . .

Birdy begins to play for the quietly attentive audience.

EXT. SCHOOL

Ed is among the crowd streaming from the gym into the warm summer night. He looks around the parking lot.

                                ED (V.O.)
. . . I could afford to charge less than the usual manager, not having to put up a big front like a lot of these phonies. And I could be with her, enough to keep myself feeling OK . . .

A trace of a frown as he spots her leaning against a car, laughing, passing a cigarette back and forth with another student – a boy.

. . . Why couldn't that work? . . . Why not? . . .

Birdy's easy smile remains as Ed approaches, but the boy's drops; he puts on a face more suitable for meeting adults.

                                BIRDY
Hi, Mr Crane.

                                ED
Hello, Birdy. I thought that was very good.

                                BIRDY
Oh, in there? I messed up a little bit in the scherzo. I guess, if nobody noticed, it's OK. Mr Crane, this is Tony, a friend of mine. Tony, Mr Crane.

                                ED
Hello, Tony.

                                TONY
Hello, sir.

Silence. The teens wait for the adult to direct the conversation; Ed has nothing to say. At length, he clears his throat.

ED

... Well, congratulations. I guess I'll be getting home.

TONY

Nice to meet you, sir.

TURANDOT SUITE

It is morning. We are tracking past an unmade bed toward the bathroom, where we hear water running.

ED (V.O.)

... Anyway, that's what I was thinking about in the days leading up to the trial. It seemed like once that was over, I'd be ready for a new start. Freddy Riedenschneider was very optimistic. He was busy preparing ...

We have rounded the open bathroom door to find Riedenschneider hunched over the sink, toothbrush in hand, spitting out water. He rises, looks at himself in the mirror, sprinkles some tonic in his hair.

... And finally it came ... the first day of the trial ...

Riedenschneider runs his fingers through his hair.

... What Riedenschneider called the Big Show.

He straightens his tie, gives his neck a twist.

COURTROOM

We are close on the back of Riedenschneider's gleaming hair. He is sitting at the defense table.

There is the murmur of a crowd that has yet to be called to order.

FRANK

Where's the judge? How come there's no judge?

Ed and Frank sit next to each other in the first gallery row directly behind Riedenschneider.

... Where's the judge, Ed?

Ed shrugs. Frank looks at Riedenschneider's back.

. . . How come the judge doesn't come out?

RIEDENSCHNEIDER

The judge comes in last. He'll come in when Doris gets here.

FRANK

So where's Doris? I thought we started at ten. Hey, Rieden-schneider, where's Doris?

Riedenschneider is curt:

RIEDENSCHNEIDER

She's late.

FRANK

Late? How can she be late?

Riedenschneider doesn't answer; Frank turns to Ed.

. . . She's in prison, Ed. None of *us* are in prison, and yet we're not late. We're on time, Ed. How can Doris be late? What, they don't have wake-up calls?

The murmur of the crowd subsides as a door behind the judge's bench opens and the judge hurriedly enters.

The gallery rises but the judge quickly waves them back down and, rather than seating himself, leans forward over his desk to give a peremptory beckoning wave to Riedenschneider and the prosecutor.

JUDGE

Counselors.

Riedenschneider, puzzled, approaches the bench, as does his counterpart from the other table. The judge, still leaning forward, speaks to them in a low voice that is not audible from the gallery.

The crowd has started murmuring again, also in hushed tones. Frank leans in toward Ed.

FRANK

What's going on, Ed? I thought there would be arguments. The bailiff, and so forth . . .

Ed, also puzzled, is watching Riedenschneider, who suddenly stiffens. As the judge continues to talk, Riedenschneider looks back over his shoulder at Ed.

. . . Ed, what is this? Is this procedure?

The two lawyers nod at the judge and walk back to their respective tables. The judge now summons a uniformed man standing to one side.

JUDGE

Bailiff.

As the judge and the bailiff confer, Riedenschneider looks down at his desk and, for something to do, straightens various papers.

RIEDENSCHNEIDER

I don't understand . . . We had a real shot at it . . . We could have won this thing . . .

The bailiff announces:

BAILIFF

In the matter of the State of California versus Doris Crane, Case Number 87249 assigned to this Superior Court . . .

As the bailiff drones, Riedenschneider shakes his head.

RIEDENSCHNEIDER

. . . It doesn't make any sense . . .

[handwritten: shot of gavel as it hits — cut to elevator strings]

BARBERSHOP

Late afternoon sun slants in.

The shop, not open for business, is very still. Ed, in his courtroom suit, sits in one of the vinyl chairs that line one wall, hunched forward, forearms on his knees.

Frank, also still in his suit, is up in one of the barber chairs, one hand cupped to his forehead, weeping.

ED (V.O.)

She'd hanged herself. I'd brought her a dress to wear to court and she'd used the belt. I didn't understand it either. At first I thought maybe it had something to do with me, that she'd figured out somehow how I fit into it and couldn't stand it, couldn't stand knowing . . .

BEDROOM

Night. Ed is in bed, staring at the ceiling.

ED (V.O.)

. . . That wasn't it, I would find out later. For now, everything just seemed ruined . . .

METROPOLE LOBBY

Riedenschneider is at the cashier's desk, checking out. Behind him a bellman's cart is piled high with his bags.

ED (V.O.)

. . . Freddy Riedenschneider went back to Sacramento still shaking his head, saying it was the biggest disappointment of his professional career . . .

FRANK'S HOUSE

Day. Frank's kitchen.

Frank sits at his kitchen table, staring, in a bathrobe thrown over his pyjamas, unshaven.

ED (V.O.)
. . . Frankie fell to pieces. I suspect he was drinking; anyway, he stopped coming in to work . . .

BARBERSHOP

Ed, in his smock, works on a customer.

ED (V.O.)
. . . That left me to keep the place going, or the bank would've taken it.

As he uses the electric clippers, a cigarette plumes between his lips. He squints against the smoke drifting past his eyes.

. . . *I* was the principal barber now. I hired a new man for the second chair . . .

Ed's former chair is indeed being manned by a newcomer, a gangly young man who animatedly chats up his customer.

. . . I'd hired the guy who did the least gabbing when he came in for an interview. But I guess the new man had only kept quiet because he was nervous; once he had the job, he talked from the minute I opened the shop in the morning . . .

EXT. BARBERSHOP

It is evening. Ed is locking the barbershop as, next to him on the side-walk, the new man continues to chat, gesticulating to illustrate his story.

ED (V.O.)
. . . until I locked up at night. For all I know, he talked to himself on the way home.

STREET

Ed walks along the sidewalk.

[handwritten: tracking him thru crowds against them]

ED (V.O.)

. . . When *I* walked home, it seemed like everyone avoided looking at me . . .

Indeed, none of the passers-by establish eye contact; their averted eyes make the crowd a faceless throng.

. . . as if I'd caught some disease. This thing with Doris, nobody wanted to talk about it; it was like I was a ghost walking down the street . . .

HOUSE

As Ed lets himself in.

ED (V.O.)

. . . And when I got home now, the place felt empty.

He sits on the couch and, after a beat, takes a cigarette pack from his pocket and taps out a smoke.

. . . I sat in the house, but there was nobody there. I was a ghost; I didn't see anyone; no one saw me . . .

BARBERSHOP

Ed is in his smock again, operating the clippers.

ED (V.O.)

. . . I was the barber.

FADE OUT

The drone of the clippers has continued over the black. A voice fades up:

[handwritten: Ed looking at alien story in LIFE]

VOICE 1

So two blocks later I look at the change she gave me and, golly, I'm two bits short.

VOICE 2

Two bits short.

VOICE 1

So I walk back over to Linton's, find this gal – big argument; she doesn't even recall the transaction.

78

VOICE 2

No recollection.

VOICE 1

Doesn't recall the transaction, no recollection, so I said,
Look, dear . . .

FADE IN

*We are looking at a magazine story. Its headline, over an illustration of
a cresting wave, is:* WAVE OF THE FUTURE.

*Underneath are black-and-white photographs of heavy equipment and
racks of clothing on motorized tracks. Subheadlines read:* NEXT TO
GODLINESS – Dry Cleaning Sweeps the Nation – The Thoroughly
Modern Way to Clean.

Ed sits in one of the vinyl chairs, staring at Life *magazine. The offscreen conversation drones on as the new man works on his customer.*

NEW MAN

. . . go ahead, look at the menu, if you're in before six o'clock
it's the, whatchamacallit, the –

CUSTOMER

Early Bird Special.

NEW MAN

What? Yeah, the Early Riser . . .

*Ed flips the pages of the magazine, and stops on a photograph of a
dark desert landscape with one bright light hovering in the sky. The
caption underneath:* ROSWELL, NEW MEXICO.

VOICE

Crane?

Ed looks up.

*A man in a black suit and fedora has directed the question at the new
man, who looks up from his gabbling, momentarily slackjawed.*

ED

. . . I'm Crane.

                              MAN
My name is Diedrickson. County medical examiner.

                              ED
Yeah?

                          DIEDRICKSON
Just came for an informal chat . . .

Diedrickson looks around uncomfortably.

        . . . Why don't I buy you a drink?

*Ed rises from his chair and, as he unbuttons his smock, addresses the
new man, who still gapes.*

                              ED
Dwight, you OK here for a few minutes?

                           DWIGHT
Whuh – uh, yeah, sure Ed, take your time.

BAR

It is late afternoon, dusty and empty.

*Ed and Diedrickson sit on adjacent stools, Diedrickson cocking his hat
lower to its man-sitting-at-a-bar position.*

As the bartender approaches:

                          DIEDRICKSON
Rye.

                              ED
Just coffee.

                          DIEDRICKSON
You sure you don't want something stiffer?

Ed shrugs and shakes his head.

                          BARTENDER
 Coffee it is.

*He leaves. Diedrickson interlaces his fingers on the bartop and stares at
them. After a beat:*

Ed is lit from behind — his profile with fedora + smoke is silouetted

DIEDRICKSON

. . . County M. E. does an autopsy on anyone who dies in custody. I don't know if you knew that. It's routine.

Ed doesn't answer. Diedrickson, after some more staring at his hands, plows on:

. . . Doesn't become a matter of public record unless there's foul play. However. I don't believe I'm *prohibited* from telling you this. I guess I'm not obliged to tell you, either. I don't exactly know. But if *I* were the man, I'd want to be told.

ED

Told what?

DIEDRICKSON

I, uh . . . thanks.

The bartender has set down the drinks.

Diedrickson waits for him to leave. He takes a hit from his glass. Finally:

. . . I'm sorry to add to your burden, Crane, but *I'd* want to know if it was me. Your wife was pregnant. First trimester.

A pause.

. . . Well, there it is.

Another pause.

. . . I'm sorry.

He mutters to himself:

. . . Hell, I hope I've done the right thing.

ED

My wife and I had not . . . performed the sex act in many years.

Diedrickson stiffens.

DIEDRICKSON
(*murmuring*)

. . . Jesus.

81

(*aloud*)

. . . Well, that's not really my business.

He is hastily digging for money.

. . . I'm sorry. Well, there it is.

He leaves a couple of bills on the bar and mumbles as he leaves:

. . . Good luck, Crane.

His retreating footsteps echo down the bar.

APARTMENT HALLWAY

It is a dingy hallway lit by bare bulbs. Ed stands in the middle background, knocking on a door. ɯ Shadow

ED (V.O.)

Doris and I had never really talked much. I don't think that's a bad thing, necessarily. But it was funny: now I wanted to talk – now, with everyone gone. I was alone, with secrets I didn't want and no one to tell them to anyway.

The door opens and Ed is admitted by the unseen tenant.

APARTMENT

We hear a low murmuring as we slowly pan the apartment. It is overfurnished with heavy, ornate chairs, sideboards, chests too big for the space and all going to seed. Surface areas are covered with yellowing lacework or exotic brocades; the one lamp has a veil thrown over it to further scrim down its feeble light.

Our pan brings us onto Ed seated at a small card table across from a small elderly woman in a shawl who is the source of the murmuring. Her eyes are squeezed shut in concentration as she mumbles.

ED (V.O.)

I visited a woman who was supposed to have powers in communicating with those who had passed across, as she called it. She said that people who passed across were picky about who they'd communicate with, not like most people you run into on this side . . .

The woman opens her eyes and looks at Ed.

> WOMAN
> Giff me your hant.

Ed places his hand in the center of the table.

> ED (V.O.)
> . . . so you needed a guide who they didn't mind talking to,
> someone with a gift for talking to souls . . .

Ed looks at the woman's spotted and vein-lined hand as it rests upon his. Her mumbling resumes.

> . . . Well, first she told me that my wife was in a peaceful
> place, that our souls were still connected by some spiritual
> bond, that she had never stopped loving me even though
> she'd done some things she wasn't proud of . . .

Ed looks up at the old woman.

> . . . She was reading me like a book.

She is stealing a glance at Ed to check his reaction.

> . . . And then she started talking about 'Dolores' this and
> 'Dolores' that and was there anything I wanted to tell
> 'Dolores,' and I knew I'd just be telling it to the old bat. And
> even if somehow Doris could hear, it wouldn't be on account
> of this so-called medium.

APARTMENT HALLWAY

Ed is leaving.

> ED (V.O.)
> She was a phony. Just another gabber.

EXT. TENEMENT

Ed emerges from the building.

> ED (V.O.)
> I was turning into Ann Nirdlinger, Big Dave's wife. I had
> to turn my back on the old lady, on the veils, on the ghosts,

[handwritten annotation: REV shot of Ed standing in doorway – light from building casts Ed's shadow down steps]

83

on the dead, before they all sucked me in . . .

Ed disappears into the night.

ABUNDAS HOUSE

It is night. We are looking through the screen door. Walter Abundas sits in yellow lamplight by a small table to the side of the staircase, over which papers are strewn. He is murmuring into the telephone as he examines the papers, glasses halfway down his nose, a drink in one hand.

Ed's hand enters to rap on the door. Walter looks up, sets the phone down and comes to the door.

                    WALTER
   Ed, how're you holding up?

                    ED
   I'm OK, Walter, thanks.

Walter opens the door to him.

                    WALTER
   I'm so damn sorry about your loss. Terrible thing. Just damn
   terrible.

                    ED
   Yeah.

                    WALTER
   Birdy's in the ~~parlor~~ upstairs – I'm on long distance here.

                    ED
   Sure, Walter. Thanks.

PARLOR

Birdy also has papers spread across a ~~table~~ bed in front of her: homework. She looks up at Ed's entrance.

                    BIRDY
   Hello, Mr Crane.

84

ED

Hello, Birdy.

BIRDY

We haven't seen you since . . . I'm terribly sorry.

Ed sits across from her.

ED

Yeah.

BIRDY

We've certainly missed you.

ED

Birdy, I've been doing a lot of thinking. There are a lot of
things that haven't worked out for me. Life has dealt me
some bum cards . . .

He is loading a cigarette into his mouth.

. . . or maybe I just haven't played 'em right, I don't know.
But you're –

BIRDY

Pop doesn't like people smoking in here.

Ed stares. This takes a moment to register.

ED

Oh. Sorry.

Birdy lowers her voice:

BIRDY

Sometimes I have a cigarette in here when he's away. Never when he's in the house. He can smell it a mile off.

Ed is pocketing the cigarette.

ED

Sure . . . Sure, it's his house.

BIRDY

That's what he keeps telling me.

Ed smiles thinly.

ED

Anyway, uh . . . my point is you're young. A kid really, your whole life ahead of you. But it's not too soon to start thinking . . . to start making opportunities for yourself. Before it all washes away.

BIRDY

Well, sure, I guess. Pop says so too. I work pretty hard at school.

ED

That's swell. However, the music, if you want to pursue it, well, the lessons from Mrs Swan, they'll only take you so far. There's this guy in San Francisco, I've made inquiries, everybody says he's the best. Trained lots of people who've gone on to have big concert careers, symphony orchestras, the works. His name is Jacques Carcanogues. I'm not sure I'm pronouncing it right. Anyway, he's a Frenchman.

BIRDY

Boy.

ED

You've got talent, anyone could see that. And he's the best. If he thinks a student has talent, he'll take 'em on for next to nothing. You're a cinch to be accepted, I could cover the cost of the lessons, like I said, it's pretty modest –

                              BIRDY

Oh, Mr Crane –

                               ED

I have to do it. I can't stand by and watch more things go down the drain. You're young, you don't understand.

                              BIRDY

Geez, Mr Crane, I don't know. I hadn't really thought about a career or stuff.

                               ED

I know you haven't. Look, just go meet him as a favor to me. I talked to this guy. Hope I pronounced his name right. He sounded very busy, but he's not a bad egg; he loosened up a little when I told him how talented you are. He agreed to see you this Saturday. He said maybe you were a diamond in the rough. His words.

                              BIRDY

Geez, Mr Crane.

                               ED

Just see him, as a favor to me.

STUDIO WAITING ROOM

It is a small square room with straightbacked chairs set against the walls. At the far end of the room a door leads to a studio from which piano music dully emanates; it is a fast and difficult piece of music.

Ed sits waiting. He is the only adult; two or three youngsters of different ages sit apparently waiting for their lessons.

Ed looks at one of the waiting boys in a white shirt and bow tie. He is perhaps eleven. His hair is greased back in a Junior Contour.

Another boy, in a cardigan sweater, sports a Butch.

The piano piece is ending. There is the murmur of voices. Dull footsteps.

The studio door swings open.

A small man in a rumpled black suit smudged with cigarette ash is bowing Birdy out the door. He has a goatee and a knotted foulard. His eyes flit over the waiting room and settle on Ed.

CARCANOGUES

. . . You are ze fahzer?

ED

No. Uh . . . family friend.

MAN

I am Carcanogues.

He smiles at Birdy.

. . . You wait, my dear?

BIRDY

Sure, Mr K.

A jerk of Carcanogues' head bids Ed rise.

STUDIO

Ed enters, uncomfortable. He looks around, taking in the high-ceilinged space, which is dominated by a grand piano.

Carcanogues has followed him and now runs water from a tap.

CARCANOGUES

I speak to you on ze phone, non? You have a special interest in music?

ED

Uh-huh.

CARCANOGUES

Ah yes, a music lover.

ED

Well, I don't pretend to be an expert.

CARCANOGUES

Ah.

He uncaps a small bottle of pills, shakes two into his palm, tosses them back and washes them down.

. . . Ah-hah.

He twists a cigarette into a long holder, sticks it in his mouth and lights it.

. . . Mm.

ED

Well? How'd she do?

This elicits a Gallic frown of consideration.

CARCANOGUES

Ze girl? . . . She seems like a very nice girl. She *plays*, monsieur, like a very nice girl. Ztinks. Very nice girl. However, ztinks.

ED

I don't understand.

CARCANOGUES

Is not so hard to understand. Her playing, very polite.

ED

Did she make mistakes?

Another Gallic moue:

CARCANOGUES

Mistake, no, it says E-flat, she plays E-flat. Ping-ping. Hit the right note, always. Very proper.

ED

I don't understand, no mistakes, she's just a kid – I thought you taught the, uh, the –

CARCANOGUES

Ah, but that is just what I cannot teach. I cannot teach her to have the soul. Look, monsieur, play the piano, is not about the fingers. *Done* with the fingers, yes. But the music, she is inside. Inside, monsieur . . .

A two-handed gesture, indicating his heart.

89

... The music start here ...

He waggles his fingers:

... come out through here; then, maybe ...

His wave takes in the heavens:

... she can go up there.

> ED
>
> Well, look, I don't claim to be an expert –

> CARCANOGUES
>
> Then you listen to me, for I am expert. That girl, she give me a headache. She cannot play. Nice girl. Very clever hands. Nice girl. Someday, I think, maybe, she make a very good typist.

DRIVING

We are driving through the rural countryside of northern California. It is a two-lane road with little traffic. Sun strobes the car through the passing trees.

Ed drives, glaring. Birdy, next to him, seems unperturbed, even cheerful.

> BIRDY
>
> ... I stank, didn't I?

> ED
>
> He didn't say that.

> BIRDY
>
> But more or less.

> ED
>
> Look, I'm no expert, but –

> BIRDY
>
> It doesn't matter, Mr Crane.

> ED
>
> I'm sure there's a dozen teachers better than this clown. More qualified. Goddamn phony.

BIRDY

But it doesn't matter. Really. I'm not interested in playing music professionally.

Ed looks at her.

. . . I'm not certain I'll have a career at all, and if I do, I'll probably be a veterinarian.

ED

. . . Uh-huh.

BIRDY

I do appreciate the interest you've taken, though.

ED

Ah . . . it's nothing.

BIRDY

I'm only sorry that I didn't play better for you. I know it would've made you happy. You know what you are?

ED

Huh.

BIRDY

You're an enthusiast.

ED

Huh. Yeah. Maybe . . .

He loads a cigarette into his mouth.

. . . I guess I've been all wet.

BIRDY

But I do appreciate it, Mr Crane . . .

She reaches over to touch his thigh.

. . . I wanted to make you happy.

ED

Birdy –

BIRDY

It's OK . . .

She is leaning over his lap.

. . . I want to do it, Mr Crane.

Ed is shocked:

ED

Birdy!

He reaches awkwardly, wanting to push her away but not wanting to be violent.

. . . No, please.

BIRDY

Please, Mr Crane, it's OK, please –

The blare of an oncoming horn.

Ed looks up, one hand struggling with Birdy, the other on the wheel.

The oncoming car.

Ed swerves, tires screech into a skid, Birdy screams.

CRASH: *the car hits a roadside tree.*   camera spins

BLACK.

ED (V.O.)

Time slows down right before an accident, and I had time to think about things. I thought about what an undertaker had told me once – that your hair keeps growing, for a while any-way, after you die . . .   car flies thru air

A hubcap is skipping in slow motion along the road and then off the road, down an embankment.   slow mo

. . . And then it stops. I thought, what keeps it growing? Is it like a plant in soil? What goes out of the soil? The soul? And when does the hair realize that it's gone?

We are high, looking down at Ed, who is motionless, head resting on the steering wheel of the stopped car. We boom down toward him, slowly rotating as we move in. As we move we lose focus; Ed becomes more and more blurry.

92

The blurry shape is now slowly spinning away from us, a bright revolving disc spinning up into the darkness until it disappears, leaving only black.

FADE IN

Ed sits on the front porch of his bungalow, smoking a cigarette in the late afternoon light.

A dog barks next door; a distant screen door slams; children are playing somewhere up the street.

Ed looks down at his watch. It is 5.30.

Something attracts his attention: at the foot of his driveway stands a man in a cream-colored suit and hat. He is a small figure, perfectly still, staring at the gravel driveway.

After a beat he lifts up a small clipboard, squints at the house, and jots something down.

He finishes writing, screws the lid back onto his pen, and is sticking it into a breast pocket when he realizes he is being watched. His manner instantly warms.

MAN

Hello!

ED

Hello.

The man starts up the walk.

MAN

I notice you still have peastone in your driveway.

ED

Yeah.

MAN

Well, of course, you have to rejuvenate that once every couple of years, don't you, when the peastone thins out.

Ed shrugs.

. . . Where does it go, huh? Like the odd sock. But you *know*

93

where it goes – you probably pick pieces of it off your lawn all the time, churn it up with your lawn mower, sweep it off the walk here – pain in the neck.

Ed shrugs again.

ED

Doesn't bother me.

MAN

Well, have you ever considered tar Macadam? People think it's just for public works and commercial purposes, roads, parking lots, so forth . . .

A car pulls into the drive.

. . . but we have the technology now to bring it to the home-owner, the individual consumer, at a very reasonable price.

Doris emerges from the car.

. . . Mind if I show you the specifications? – Evening, ma'am.

Doris gives him a hard look.

DORIS

What're *you* selling?

The man gives a practiced laugh.

MAN

Well, ma'am, I was just telling your husband here about tar Macadam, for your home driveway here – these are the specs . . .

Doris takes the brochure he has pulled from a small case.

. . . It's the modern way to –

Doris tears the brochure in half and hands it back.

DORIS

Get lost. Strong woman

The man gazes at her. His smile fades fast and he and Doris stare at each other, two hard cases.

94

He turns stiffly and stalks off.

Once his gaze has broken, Doris turns as well. She stalks up the stairs to the porch and bangs through the screen front door of the house, letting it slam behind her.

Quiet, early evening.

Ed sits, smoking.

At length he rises and goes into the house.

INT. BUNGALOW

It is dim, no lights on yet. We hear banging and clomping from the kitchen.

Doris emerges with a clinking sound, chasing ice cubes around a drink with a swizzle stick. Her face is still hard-set.

With a groan of its old upholstery springs she sits onto the couch.

Ed sits as well. He draws on his cigarette, drags an ashtray closer on the coffee table.

She sips. He puffs.

ED
. . . Doris –

DORIS
Nah, don't say anything. I'm all right.

They sit. The light is failing. The clink of ice cubes.

FADE OUT   hub cap turns into doctors
                      head light

In the black we hear machine noise of indistinct origin. As the noise becomes more defined we also hear shouting, faint, distant:

VOICE
Are you there? Are you awake?

A blurry white disc is fading up. As it focuses it resolves into the reflector worn by a white-robed doctor, leaning in close.

He leans away, murmuring:

95

DOCTOR

He's coming around. Can you talk, sir? These men have to
talk.

*Ed is lying in a hospital bed. His face is bandaged and one side is
grotesquely swollen. The machine noise is life support.*

. . . Sir? Are you awake? He's awake.

Two police officers, Persky and Krebs, lean in.   P. O. V

PERSKY

Are you awake? . . . Is he awake?

KREBS

Crane? We have to tell you, as soon as you're conscious – is
he conscious?

PERSKY

His eyes are open.

KREBS

Uh . . . you're under arrest.

PERSKY

As soon as the doctor lets us, we gotta move you. Does he
understand that? We're supposed to tell him. Are you conscious?

KREBS

You'll go to the prison hospital.

PERSKY

Under arrest for murder.

Ed's speech is thickened by injuries and anesthesia:

ED

Birdy . . . I didn't mean to –

KREBS

What'd he say?

ED

Birdy . . .

96

DOCTOR

Birdy. The girl. No, the girl's OK. Broken clavicle.

The doctor leans in.

. . . That's the collarbone, Crane. Broken. She's OK though.

KREBS

So he understands? He's under arrest for murder?

ED

Big Dave.

PERSKY

Huh?

KREBS

What'd he say? Does he understand?

PERSKY

He said OK. Is that what he said?

Krebs raises his voice:

KREBS

You're under arrest for the murder of Creighton Tolliver! Do you understand?

The voices are fading away:

PERSKY

. . . Does he understand? . . .

FADE OUT.

UNDERWATER

Light glimmers in water. We are drifting down, down, down.

We bring in languidly waving arms – the arms of a child, waving to keep himself submerged. It is a ten-year-old boy staring, wide-eyed, at something in front of him. Bubbles intermittently stream from his open mouth.

ED (V.O.)

The pansy. A kid diving at a waterhole outside of town had found his car . . .

The reverse shows the car, also submerged, with Creighton Tolliver inside, also wide-eyed, his hairpiece attached at only one corner, the rest of it waving free.

. . . They'd winched it out . . .

TRACKING

We are tracking laterally across a line of faces: seated men. The men rise.

chance

ED (V.O.)

. . . and found he'd been beaten, just like Big Dave said – beaten to death . . .

FATE

We arc around a judge entering the chamber through the small door behind his raised bench.

. . . Inside his briefcase were the partnership papers I'd signed . . .

The judge seats himself and we resume our lateral track on the jury, now reseating itself.

. . . showing that I'd given him ten grand. For the district attorney . . .

In response to a prompt from the judge the district attorney rises to read the charge. His voice plays distantly, muted, the words not discernible under the continuing voice-over.

. . . that made it fall into place: I'd gotten Doris to steal the money, the pansy had gotten wise somehow, and I'd had to kill him to cover my tracks. I was in a spot. I called in Freddy Riedenschneider . . .

Riedenschneider rises into frame at the defense table. As he listens to the charge:

. . . and signed the house over to him. He said he didn't ordinarily work that cheap, but he figured he owed me something since the last one hadn't played out . . .

The drone of the D. A. has ended and Riedenschneider's echoing voice drops into the hole:

98

RIEDENSCHNEIDER

Not guilty, your honor . . .

ED (V.O.)

I tried to tell him the whole story, but Riedenschneider stopped me. He said the story made his head hurt, and anyway he didn't see any way of using it without putting me on the hot seat for the murder of Big Dave . . .

Riedenschneider claps Ed reassuringly on the shoulder as he sits next to him. Ed still wears a cast on one arm and one leg.

. . . He told me not to worry, though, said he'd think of something, Freddy Riedenschneider wouldn't let me down.

JAIL

We are tracking in on Ed, lying on the bunk in his cell.

ED (V.O.)

. . . They put me on twenty-four-hour deathwatch . . .

A reverse track shows a guard on a tilted-back straightbacked chair, outside the cell door, staring at Ed.

. . . so that I couldn't Cheat Justice like they said my wife had done . . .

COURTROOM

The district attorney is rising again, this time to address the jury.

ED (V.O.)

. . . But in front of the jury they had it that Doris was a saint; the whole plan had been mine, I was a Svengali who'd forced Doris to join my criminal enterprise . . .

The district attorney is pointing at Ed.

DISTRICT ATTORNEY

. . . cynically used his own wife as a cat's paw in a scheme of diabolical cunning . . .

ED (V.O.)

On and on it went, how I'd used Doris and then let her take

the fall. That stuff smarted because some of it was close to
being true . . .

*The district attorney seats himself. The jury's eyes turn to Freddy
Riedenschneider, who studies the tabletop in front of him, either digest-
ing the D. A.'s opening statement, or seeking inspiration for his own.*

. . . And then it was Riedenschneider's turn.

Riedenschneider rises, paces, begins to talk.

. . . I gotta hand it to him, he tossed a lot of sand in their eyes.
He talked about how I'd lost my place in the universe . . .

RIEDENSCHNEIDER
. . . a puny player on the great world's stage . . .

ED (V.O.)
. . . how I was too ordinary to be the criminal mastermind
the D. A. made me out to be, how there was some greater
scheme at work that the state had yet to unravel, and he
threw in some of the old truth stuff he hadn't had a chance
to trot out for Doris . . .

RIEDENSCHNEIDER
. . . who among us is in a position to say . . .

ED (V.O.)
. . . He told them to look at me – look at me close. That the
closer they looked the less sense it would all make, that I
wasn't the kind of guy to kill a guy, that I was the barber, for
Christ's sake . . .

We pan the jury, solemnly listening to Riedenschneider.

. . . I was just like them, an ordinary man, guilty of living in a
world that had no place for me, guilty of wanting to be a dry
cleaner, sure, but not of murder . . .

*Riedenschneider is striding energetically into the foreground to point a
finger directly at Ed's face.*

. . . He said I *was* Modern Man, and if they voted to convict
me, well, they'd be practically cinching the noose around
their own necks. He told them to look not at the facts but at

the meaning of the facts, and then he said the facts *had* no meaning. It was a pretty good speech, and even had me going . . .

A tap on his shoulder turns Ed around.

. . . until Frankie interrupted it.

Frank socks Ed, sending him clattering to the floor.

A bailiff immediately restrains him, but Frank looms over Ed, bellowing through tears:

FRANK
What kind of man *are* you? What kind of man *are* you?

Riedenschneider interposes his body between Frank's and Ed's, loudly protesting:

RIEDENSCHNEIDER
Move for a mistrial, your honor! Move for a mistrial! This outrageous display cannot help but prejudice . . .

Ed moves to get up, but Riedenschneider, with a sidelong glance and furtive gesture, motions for him to stay on the floor.

. . . and inflame the passions of these twelve fine men and women . . .

ED (V.O.)
. . . Well, he got his mistrial, but the well had run dry. There was nothing left to mortgage; Riedenschneider went home and the court appointed Lloyd Garroway . . .

Ed is now standing next to a distinguished older gentleman who enters the plea in the new trial:

GARROWAY
Your honor, we plead guilty, with extenuating circumstances.

ED (V.O.)
. . . who threw me on the mercy of the court. It was my only chance, he said. I guess that meant I never had a chance . . .

The judge starts droning the sentence:

JUDGE
. . . a menace to society . . . a predator on his own wife, his business associates, on an innocent young girl . . . social contract . . . line crossed . . . the offender forfeits the right to his own life . . . I hereby order that you be taken to a place of confinement . . .

PRISON HALLWAY

We are tracking down the hall.

ED (V.O.)
He wasn't buying any of that Modern Man stuff, or the uncertainty stuff, or any of the mercy stuff either. No, he was going by the book, and the book said I got the chair . . .

Ed is in the cell at the end of the hall, lying on his bunk, hands clasped behind his head.

. . . so here I am. At first I didn't know how I got here. I knew step by step of course, which is what I've told you, step by step; but I couldn't see any pattern . . .

LATER

Ed sits at the little table next to his bunk, writing.

Double
Indemnity?

ED (V.O.)
. . . Now that I'm near the end, I'm glad that this men's
magazine paid me to tell my story. Writing it has helped me
sort it all out. They're paying five cents a word, so you'll
pardon me if sometimes I've told you more than you wanted
to know . . .

Recent issues of the magazine, Gent, *and its sister publication* Nugget
lie on the little desk. Their lurid covers depict feature stories like I WAS
ABDUCTED BY ALIENS *and* AFTER TEN YEARS OF NORMAL LIFE, I
DISCOVER I AM AN ESCAPED LUNATIC.

. . . But now, all the disconnected things seem to hook up.

Ed sets aside the pen, lies down on his bunk, and closes his eyes.

right on
face

. . . That's the funny thing about going away, knowing the
date that you're gonna die – and the men's magazine wanted
me to tell how that felt . . .

We hear a pulsing treble hum. Ed opens his eyes.

The door to his cell is open.

He rises and goes through the door.

PRISON HALLWAY

Ed, alone, walks down the hallway. The pulsing treble hum is louder.

ED (V.O.)
. . . Well, it's like pulling away from the maze. While you're in
the maze you go through willy-nilly, turning where you think
you have to turn, banging into the dead ends, one thing after
another . . .

PRISON YARD

*Ed emerges into the empty prison yard ringed by high stone walls. A
hard spotlight shines down from above. Ed squints into it.*

ED (V.O.)

... But get some distance on it, and all those twists and turns, why, they're the shape of your life. It's hard to explain ...

The spotlight is from a hovering flying saucer. We see its revolving underside and, as it irregularly cants, a bit of its top bubble.

After spinning briefly, it tips and flies away, carrying the tremolo hum with it.

... But seeing it whole gives you some peace.

Ed turns and re-enters the prison.

ED'S CELL

Ed is lying on his bunk, eyes closed, hands clasped behind his head. A hand enters to shake him awake.

Three men loom over him: two guards and another man wearing a surplice and holding a Bible.

ED (V.O.)

... The men's magazine also asked about remorse. Yeah, I guess I'm sorry about the pain I caused other people ...

PRISON HALLWAY

He is walking the last mile.

shot from behind with
long dark corridor
lit with ceiling
lights

ED (V.O.)

... but I don't regret anything. Not a thing. I used to. I used to regret being the barber.

A door at the end opens:

completely light /white
room

An electric chair. Straps open, and waiting.

... I don't know where I'm being taken.

Ed is placed in the chair.

... I don't know what waits for me, beyond the earth and sky. But I'm not afraid to go.

A man stoops at his feet. He has a bucket of water and a straight razor.

He waggles the razor in the water and starts shaving a patch of Ed's calf.

    . . . Maybe the things I don't understand will be clearer there, like when a fog blows away . . .

Ed watches as the razor makes the trip from his leg to the bucket of water, which begins to spot with small floating hairs.

    . . . Maybe Doris will be there.

They are strapping him in, connecting the electrodes.

    . . . And maybe there I can tell her . . .

The men withdraw.

    . . . all those things . . .

A thin man in a dark suit and a fedora stands by the switch. As he reaches for the switch, Ed looks up into the light.

    . . . they don't have words for here.